D0500608

MANAGING the DYNAMICS of CHANGE

MANAGING the DYNAMICS of CHANGE

The Fastest Path to Creating an Engaged and Productive Workforce

Jerald M. Jellison, Ph.D.

McGraw-Hill
New York Chicago San Francisco Lisbon London
Madrid Mexico City Milan New Delhi San Juan
Seoul Singapore Sydney Toronto

The McGraw·Hill Companies

1 2 3 4 5 6 7 8 9 0 DOC/DOC 0 9 8 7 6

ISBN 0-07-147044-1

This book is printed on recycled, acid-free paper containing a minimum of 50% recycled, de-inked fiber.

Library of Congress Cataloging-in-Publication Data

Jellison, Jerald M.
Managing the dynamics of change / by Jerald Jellison.
p. cm.
Includes index.
ISBN 0-07-147044-1 (alk. paper)
1. Organizational change—Management. I. Title.
HD58.8.J436 2007
658.4'06—dc22

2006004901

In gratitude to all the people I've spoken with
on campuses, in businesses, and at conferences.
Your interest, encouragement, examples, and
criticism have helped these ideas evolve.

CONTENTS

PREFACE

It's time to change how we manage change. Are you ready for a different approach? Many of us are still relying on the same model (transitions) and tools (communication and persuasion) that have been around for many decades. Would you like to learn an innovative way to think about the change process (the J Curve) and gain skill at using a completely new set of practical tools (activation) to make change happen—fast?

The older approaches still have an important place but they're limited because they don't address the fundamental problem of implementing change, which is people's emotional resistance. If you've managed during a merger, downsizing, reorganization, outsourcing, or tried to set up new processes and procedures, you know that the greatest challenge is dealing with the human dimensions of change. Anyone who thinks the higher-ups decide and the worker bees meekly comply hasn't tried to switch the brand of soda sold in the break room, let alone execute a major change.

To understand why, think of the famous line from the movie *The Godfather*—"It's business, it's not personal." That's the way many managers look at organizational change. They see change in logical and matter-of-fact business terms. Change becomes simply a good business decision based on a rational process. For the people impacted—or those targeted for elimination in the gangster movie—the change is very personal and very emotional.

Leaders tend to think, "Look, this is a business we're running. We have to adapt and change or we'll be killed by the competition. I'll just explain the logic of this and once our people understand why we have to change they'll make the switch." In your experience, how effective is rational persuasion in getting resistant people to change? While the frontline people are listening to the leader explain the reasons for the change, they're often thinking, "This is going to be terrible for me. My career and my life are going to be completely screwed up. I don't like this and I'm not going to do it." When people get frightened about a change, leaders either don't recognize or don't know how to deal with their follower's emotional reactions.

This book is for leaders at all levels of the organization—whether chief executive officers, executive vice presidents, middle managers, or frontline supervisors. It will give you clear answers and solutions to the challenges of people's resistance to change. Applications and action are the driving themes of the book. It's filled with new ideas and practical techniques, not anecdotes or war stories. You'll learn straightforward and effective tools you can use to speed the implementation of change.

Being a practical book, it isn't about *the need* for change. Nor is it about a strategy for execution. The need for change is obvious, and while it's important to have a strategic perspective, people involved in the day-to-day work of implementation need *tactics and tools*—practical techniques they can put to work immediately to get results.

These ideas are based on my experience and research. In over 30 years of leading an organization, serving as a business consultant to some of the world's premier large and small organizations, and conducting research on interpersonal influence, I've developed a new approach to helping people change.

We'll begin with a different way of understanding what happens to people as they go through the change process. The focus will be on individuals because successful implementation ultimately comes down to getting particular people to begin doing things differently. At the level of the individual we'll aim to understand exactly what people are thinking and feeling because that's the basis of the human reaction to change.

The first section presents a new way to think about change and critically reviews the tools we often use to influence people to change. Chapter 1 introduces the J Curve, which describes people's performance, thoughts, and emotions at each of the five stages of the change process. Chapter 2 is very practical; it lays out concrete ways you can use the J Curve in your work situation and how you can use it to modify your actions as a leader. Chapter 3 examines the limitations of the tools we most commonly turn to when seeking to influence people to change: communication and persuasion. You'll learn why persuasion is such a weak tool and how that causes many managers to turn to threats as a last-ditch method to force people to change. Chapter 4 introduces a new approach to change—activation—which avoids the disadvantages of persuasion and coercion by helping people to begin changing despite their doubts and anxieties.

To make certain you can start to use activation to your advantage immediately, Section 2 describes how you can begin employing each of the new tools that make up activation. In Chapter 5 you'll learn practical skills such as communicating at ground level. In Chapter 6 you will find out about asking more and telling less and about the *Jeopardy* technique. Chapter 7 explains the importance of front-loading rewards, the bamboo technique, and personalizing praise. Chapter 8 shows how to make it easy for people to start changing.

Section 3 tells you how to sustain changes within your organization. Chapter 9 details the process of creating a culture of accountability. Chapter 10 explains how to build and maintain enthusiasm for change. And the final chapter will show you practical things you can do each day to create a culture of change. This is an action-oriented book that is guaranteed to change your thinking and your success as a leader.

ACKNOWLEDGMENTS

As the dedication indicates, I'm deeply grateful to the many people who have played a role in the development of these ideas and this book. Some individuals deserve special recognition.

In the academic world, Judson Mills taught me to think and write; Devindra Singh has been a continuing friend in the study of psychology; Jared Kenworthy has been a vital intellectual companion; and Wendy Martyna taught me to value people's humanity.

In the business world, David Forman had faith in my capabilities even though they don't match his own; David Owens extended his trust and respect; Bob Zeinstra valued my message; Kate O'Keefe was a creative inspiration in teaching adults.

Gary Perez has served as a model of how a dedicated and compassionate leader can enable people to change and to build a business. I'm very grateful to the staff, board, and members of the USC Credit Union who have enabled me to learn and grow with them.

Dale Fetherling has a way with words. His perceptive editorial judgment and responsiveness was critical to the completion of this book.

Most important of all, my wife, Karen, has never wavered in her support. Her confidence enabled me to take advantage of innumerable opportunities.

MANAGING the DYNAMICS of CHANGE

SECTION

UNDERSTANDING THE CHANGE PROCESS

Chapter

TAKING A REALISTIC LOOK AT CHANGE: THE J CURVE

Like a roller coaster, change frightens even as it thrills—and often feels more like fun when it's over than when you're doing it. Change suggests progress...growth...success...and also the possibility of uncertainty, failure, and fear. The fundamental challenge of implementing change is how to help people through their fears and doubts so that they experience the joys of growth and success. Knowing how to deal with these human aspects of change is critical to your success as a manager and leader.

Often, the mere possibility that something *could* go wrong causes many workers to conclude that something (probably many things) *will* go awry. This fear produces doubts, anxiety, and resistance. In turn, these feelings become roadblocks that slow or doom the effort...*unless* you understand how change occurs, what employees think as they face change, and how to help them over the rough spots.

Begin any change and you start along a track that, again like a roller coaster, presents you with stomach-churning drops and thrilling climbs. But the workplace is not an amusement park. The stakes are higher, and the outcome is much more significant. Careers and corporate fortunes hang in the balance, so we as leaders need to know how to speed and ease the change process.

THE HUMAN DIMENSION

The J Curve provides a platform for dealing with the human dimensions of change. The letter *J* approximates the path that most major changes follow, whether it's introducing a new business process, merging mega-corporations, or changing your golf swing. First, there's a precipitous drop in performance followed by a ragged period of limited progress, and then a steep climb in performance improvement. If you understand where you and your employees are on the J Curve, you can make sense of all changes, past and present.

More importantly, you can help team members and coworkers handle change more smoothly and quickly when you understand what they're thinking and feeling. You can learn to help them with their doubts and worries as they move along the J Curve's five predictable stages.

And, of course, if they handle change smoothly and quickly, you become a stronger and more productive leader. Your peers may become mired in the daily ups and downs of implementation, but you'll be able to recognize the larger trajectory of change. As a wise participant-observer, you'll see the signs of progress and deftly nudge subordinates toward the ultimate target.

Over the past decade, progressive organizations—from Fortune 500 firms to small start-ups—have learned about the J Curve and found it an invaluable guide. These companies know that execution ultimately comes down to people. The J Curve gives leaders a new perspective into the human side of change. When you use the J Curve in conjunction with the new set of tools in Chapters 4 through 8, you'll be able to speed the process of change dramatically.

THE FIVE STAGES OF CHANGE

Change is about what happens to performance over time. Whether it's a whole business unit that's making the change or just one person, the arc of change normally follows a similar pattern. The J Curve nicely describes the pattern of progress and it looks like the illustration in Figure 1.1.

Of course, as shown in Figure 1.1, the curve is smoothed out to reveal the underlying pattern. In reality, there will be minor fluctuations—bumps and dips—in performance during each of the stages. The idealized curve summarizes net performance by subtracting the number of instances of failure from the number of successes at any point in time.

In this illustration, the plateau begins in positive territory. Even if the initial level of performance is in the negative range, the shape of the curve will be basically the same. The shape is amazingly consistent

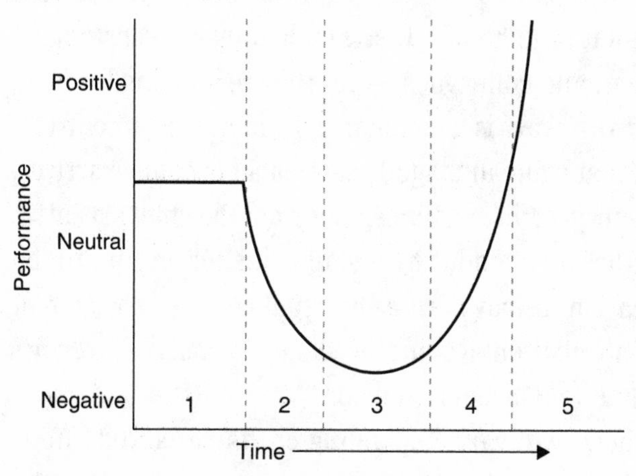

Figure 1.1 The J Curve of Change

across different change situations, except for a few minor anomalies that we'll discuss later.

THE PATH OF CHANGE

We'll take a look in detail at each of these five stages. First, we'll explore the group's *performance* during a change. Then, we'll examine people's *thoughts and feelings* as they traverse the change process. Knowing what people are thinking and feeling is a key to effectively leading your team. It's that knowledge that will enable you to speed the change process and minimize resistance.

Let's think metaphorically about the J Curve in topographical terms, starting with:

Stage 1: The Plateau

At the beginning, before the new effort gets under way, employees are on a performance plateau. Before the actual change begins, they're following established patterns. They often have a high degree of mastery of their work. And, even if they aren't masterful, they're comfortable with the routine. They've got their time-honored ways of dealing with customers, procedures, equipment, and colleagues—and they're sticking to them. "We've always done it this way" is a common refrain at this juncture.

Imagine, though, that while in Stage 1, news of a big change arrives. Maybe it comes in the form of an announcement from the chief executive officer (CEO), an offhand comment by a senior leader, or an official corporate communication. It may start as a casual comment, rumor, or purportedly insider information. No matter what the source, the news produces excitement as well as apprehension.

Reaction to the news will vary, depending on its perceived effect. News of a merger will be very appealing to those whose sphere of influence will expand, while those in the smaller firm or department that is being swallowed will have grave reservations. Similarly, news that a boss will be replaced will come as a happy relief to those who have felt his sting—or be received with regret by those who've been among his favored few.

In real-life work situations, the execution of change comes down to getting particular individuals to begin doing things differently. Therefore, we need to gain insights into what is happening at the psychological level for the people who are apprehensive about the change. There may be some people who are excited about the change, and they're easy to manage. It's those who are hesitant and resistant that we need to understand.

Resistance often appears with the announcement in Stage 1 and continues to grow as implementation moves into Stage 2. Its intensity can vary from low levels of doubt, "Well, okay, I'll give it a try, but I'm not sure it's a good idea," to defiance, "This is the dumbest idea in the world; I refuse to do it." If the target of resistance is a person, dissent may range from the diplomatic, "I'm not sure Bob, despite his technical knowledge, is the best person to head this project," to raw hostility, "Who's the bozo who came up with this?" or "Over my dead body."

In Stage 1, concerns about the impending change will take a toll on the performance of workers who are most resistant, though the work of most employees will continue at the same level. As the date for the actual launch approaches, what do people see?

A sheer cliff.

As we get closer to the cliff, attitudes and feelings become more and more intense. Thoughts are skewed to the dark side for the people with reservations. This negative frame of mind is mixed with emotions such as loss, apprehension of not being in control, and a general feeling of vulnerability.

A paramount concern for each of us when we receive news about any change is how it will affect us. "What's in this for me?" If the change seems as if it will benefit us (e.g., new advancement opportunities or greater job security), we excitedly embrace it. If it appears to diminish our standing or make our lives harder (more work, less free time, increased responsibility without increased pay), we raise our defenses. This resistance gets expressed in our private thoughts along these lines:

"This is ridiculous because..."
"This will never work."
"Whose crazy idea was this?"
"I liked things the old way."
"This is going to cost me."

Those are internal responses. Externally, though, what we say usually is geared to the business merits of the proposed change. Trying to act like good team players, we often resort to questions rather than assertions, such as:

"Why do we have to do this?"
"Where has it been tried before?"
"What problems have come up when others have tried this?"
"How will this impact our other operations?"

People often use these rational-sounding questions and arguments to disguise their lack of confidence in their own ability to successfully make the change. But, make no mistake, the underlying concern is not so much "Will this be good for the business?" Rather, it is "Will this be good for me? Will I be able to succeed?" The concerned worker often raises "business" objections rather than admit doubts about his or her own ability, for example, "I'm not sure I can do this."

What happens when employees ask you *why* a change is needed? As a responsible manager, you probably try to provide logical, fact-based answers. You're thinking that if you can explain the logic behind the change, the questioner will nod in agreement and happily go along with the program. So you lay out the details of the new technology, explaining how everyone will be better able to manage inventory and gain a competitive advantage over the firms in the marketplace.

However, the truth is you're answering the publicly stated query, probably not the real one. The real question is more along the lines of "Why are you doing this to *me*?" or "Will *I* still have a job?" or "What is *my* future with this firm?" And the inquiring employee usually will listen only well enough to comprehend a few of your reasons, so he or she can launch immediate rebuttals. His goal is not really dialogue at this point but fending off the change. His questions, like his arguments, are often driven by fear.

Not all questions or disagreements are exclusively fear-based. Some may be reasonable and worthy of being treated seriously, and it's important that you remain alert to the motive behind the question. Does the query spring from well-reasoned objections or from underlying emotional reluctance?

Another possible reaction to the announcement of an upcoming change is to deny that it will actually come to pass. Workers may convince themselves the change isn't imminent. By denying the reality, they are able to temporarily avoid their fear. Their self-deception can be so complete that when the change is launched, they'll claim they were never told about it. Interestingly, it's often the people who will be most affected by the change who will be most surprised.

Such repression may seem extreme. However, before labeling these people as crazy, it's humbling to recognize that almost all of us often do something similar. Think of how you have reacted to a brief and sharp physical pain. Many of us tell ourselves the sensation in our chest or back is only a minor reaction to stress and we can therefore ignore it. "Aw, it's nothing. Everybody gets little aches and pains when they're under pressure." We deny the reality of the pain in order to avoid the trauma we fear will result from a visit to a doctor where the diagnosis might be serious.

After the change has been announced in the second half of Stage 1, strong emotions shoot to the surface for the resisters. The dominant emotions of fear and anxiety result from anticipation of the bad things the change may bring: the things we think we'll lose, what will happen if the change doesn't work, and what will result if we're unable to perform satisfactorily? Helping people overcome this fear is critical to implementing change. We'll discuss it in detail later.

The fear sometimes leads to feelings of anger. This hostility is aimed primarily at our immediate superiors, who are "making us change" and less so at the people at the top who decided to make the change. Typically, the messenger becomes the whipping boy. Because the senior executives are often insulated from the sting of this kind of criticism, they usually underestimate the level of employees' negativity.

Although most resistance is associated with having to do something brand new, it can also appear when the change is a familiar one. In some cases employees know they could successfully implement the change and they even know the change is for the best; however, they'd rather not. A midlevel manager, for instance, may have successfully gone through similar changes in the past, so she knows she will be able to complete this one. She may even understand how the new plan will improve the organization's performance and could ultimately benefit her personally. But her bones also remember the weariness of the long hours required, the pain of her frustrations, and the impact all of this will have on her and her family. She knows she could make the change happen; she just dreads doing it again.

You've probably experienced this sense of dread in your personal life. Have you ever made a New Year's commitment to regular, early morning exercise and then three weeks later had an internal dialogue with yourself as you lie in bed on a winter morning? A part of you is saying how nice it feels to lie there, and another part urges you to keep your promise and get up and exercise. The first voice gently reminds you of how warm it is beneath the blankets and how cold it is outside. The sterner voice reiterates your pledge to exercise no matter what the obstacles. It asks you to think about how good you'll feel psychologically about having honored your commitment and how good you'll feel physically after the workout. In this debate, you know you're capable of getting out of bed to do the exercise, but your body doesn't want to endure the pain and the work.

In the workplace, this dread of executing is especially likely when employees are already swamped by, say, the new scheduling process that's linked to the new pay-for-performance system that's made worse by the inadequate training manual. Being overtaxed by the demands of multiple changes can sap anyone's energy. If a worker wasn't already overextended, he or she probably would have the energy to implement the change.

Facing change is similar to approaching the edge of an emotional cliff. As you inch closer to the rim, apprehension grows. The risk-reward analysis gets even more skewed, and undifferentiated anxiety turns into specific fears and even terror. For small changes with less potential for loss, the apprehension won't be as strong. But even seemingly insignificant change can produce uncertainty, worry, and turmoil.

When we don't know exactly what a change will mean for us, we fill the information vacuum by imagining the negative things that could happen. Remember what it was like as a child to learn to sleep in the dark? Up until now the hall light was left on or there was a night-light. Then came the fateful, life-changing night when you had to sleep without even the dimmest of lights. Lying there in utter darkness, you feared what? It wasn't really the unknown or even the dark. It was what you *knew*, or thought you knew, was out there in the dark—monsters, ghosts, bogeymen. Not only did you know they were out there, you probably knew where they were—under the bed or in the closet—and you knew they were going to do unspeakably terrible things to you.

Just as children react to the unknown of darkness by filling in the void with demons, so do we as adults anticipate that business changes will bring very real monsters to thwart our well-being. Standing on the plateau of Stage 1 and anticipating going over that emotional cliff and falling down through Stage 2, we're convinced monsters lurk there to do us grave harm. We make the unknown real by inventing things to fear.

"They're expecting the impossible."
"I won't have any autonomy."
"There goes my promotion."
"My salary probably will be reduced."
"I'll lose my job—and then the house, the car, the kids' education, and my retirement."

It doesn't take long before we picture ourselves begging on street corners or going hat in hand to a gloating in-law to ask for a loan.

It's true that most change does involve more work, at least initially. But those afraid of change often exaggerate to inhuman levels the amount of toil the change will demand. "I'm going to have to completely rearrange my entire schedule," they say. Or "I'm going to have to work 24/7 to get this done. It's impossible." Having conjured up these horrifying pictures, we'll say anything to avoid changing and that's why so many of the arguments that resisters put forward aren't completely logical.

Other people's fears may seem irrational to you, yet they are very real to them and they need to be treated respectfully. Later, we'll look at specific techniques you can use to help people with their fears.

Stage 2: The Cliff

The second stage begins when employees, many feeling as if they've got a gun in their back, step into the abyss and actually try to start to do things the new way. Maybe this means using new software, reporting to a different supervisor, learning to operate a new piece of equipment, adopting a new procedure, or the first meeting with your counterparts in the firm that just acquired yours.

And, of course, what happens when we do something that is radically different from what we've done in the past? Performance drops sharply. The Stage 1 pattern is reversed: failures now outpace successes. This is not surprising, as anyone who has taken up a new sport can attest. The novice skier falls a lot, the fledgling golfer shanks into the rough, and the new fly fisherman snags every tree branch within range.

During this stage, employees make one error after another. They can't remember the new procedures; they use the wrong words or inappropriate tools. Correct responses are few and mistakes accumulate because training was inadequate, management hasn't provided enough resources, decision making is inconsistent or nonexistent. New turf battles erupt. The net effect: performance and productivity go down, down, down.

Even if the new approach is very similar to the old way of doing things, people still make some mistakes as they adjust to the new way. And here's the general rule: the greater the difference between the new way of doing things and the old way, the greater the drop in performance.

This is also the stage where the resistance becomes intense. Dissent is now more open and vociferous.

When workers begin to do something new and different, their performance drops. Those errors fuel a new set of thoughts and feelings that build on those from Stage 1. Remember those employees in Stage 1 who were asking, "Why do we have to change?" You can guess what they're saying now, and you probably even know their tone of voice. With great self-righteousness and some finger-pointing, they remind you, "I told you so."

As the problems accumulate, you hear:

"I knew this wasn't going to work."
"It's only going to get worse."
"We're doomed."

As their thoughts turn more negative, so do their emotions. Employees now feel they're failures because they don't have a sense of control. Fear can grow into a sense of panic. They want to escape from this terrible situation.

When the new way isn't working, an alternative almost always surfaces. "Let's go back to the old way of doing things. It may not have been perfect, but it was better than this." The allure of the past grows stronger. The good old days of Stage 1 suddenly look like paradise. People who were merely skeptical about the new approach may now become resisters too.

This glorification of the old way can be disturbing to the manager. If you think about it, however, you probably can reflect on a parallel situation in your personal life. Haven't you bought a product, automobile, or home and experienced buyer's remorse? You can't figure out how to use the device, or you're worried about how you'll make the payments or how you'll deal with the unexpected maintenance issues. In those moments of doubt, you begin thinking the purchase was a bad idea.

Stage 3: The Valley

As the employees enter Stage 3, things start bottoming out. Errors aren't as frequent or as large, and workers are starting to do more things correctly. As they begin to master, for example, some of the basics of the new software program, they gradually complete more tasks successfully. They still make many mistakes. However, they tend to catch them and correct them quickly. They learn to execute one new command after another, and the performance curve turns upward as successes begin to outnumber mistakes. This is the stage during which you can observe the transition that takes place between the old and new ways of doing things.

Stage 3's valley may be short and jagged, more like a gorge, or broad and rolling like a plain that seems to go on forever. If the change is a good one, the curve eventually turns up and continues to climb. In reality, not every change sweeps upward. We'll talk about those later.

In the first half of Stage 3, net performance is still decreasing but at a much slower rate than before. The negativity of employees' emotions also decreases. Though their worst fears are quelled, they still feel uncertain. Yet as time goes by, successes accumulate and workers feel relieved that the freefall has stopped. Maybe they even feel a glimmer of hope.

In the early phase of Stage 3, managers perceive progress very differently from those who are attempting to implement the change. When you, as a manager, see employees making fewer mistakes, you may say, "Great! You're getting it." But the worker, who is still making many errors, doesn't think he's getting it. His reaction probably is along the lines of "Got what?"

"Keep doing what you just did," you advise, and the employee can't even remember what he just did. Then when the employee becomes aware that he's making fewer errors, he often attributes it to luck rather than mastery. What looks like progress to the manager still feels like a lack of control to the rank and filers because they focus more on what they're doing wrong while the manager seizes on what they're doing right.

In the second half of Stage 3, workers begin to achieve some consistency. As successes begin to now outnumber failures, employees turn cautiously optimistic. Although still not brimming with confidence, they think, "Maybe I can, sort of, do this."

Stage 4: The Ascent

In this stage, performance improves impressively. The curve rises almost as rapidly as the earlier descent. Why? Because the workers sharpen their skills, establish new procedures, eliminate inefficiencies, and coordinate better with one another. Not only are they doing things better but they're getting a psychological boost from their newfound proficiency. Their success becomes self-reinforcing and motivating.

Employees' attitudes about the new way of doing things changes dramatically as their performance climbs in Stage 4.

> "This isn't so hard."
> "I'm better than I thought I was."
> "This is kind of fun."
> "I think I can actually figure out a faster way to do this."

One clear way to tell if employees are psychologically in Stage 4 is by observing how they deal with problems. Back in Stage 2 when they encountered an obstruction, they interpreted it as a sure sign that the new way was going to be a disaster. They were ready to give up immediately. As the curve begins to climb, people respond to the problem as a solvable challenge and they hunt for constructive ways to deal with it. "This is only a minor setback," they say. "We can find a way around it."

Feelings also soar with the improving performance. Optimism replaces fear and uncertainty. "This could really work." Each success produces pleasure and makes people feel good about what they're doing. They stop resisting the change and now begin to openly accept it.

This ascent can be dramatic. The performance curve climbs and transforms a collection of individuals into a cohesive team. The work group struggled through Stages 2 and 3. Their failures brought criticism from skeptical peers. But now in Stage 4, the change is working. Pride springs from the fundamental idea of "We did it." In this crucible of change, many employees form friendships that will last a lifetime. Later, they may look back on this as one of the most deeply satisfying times of their careers.

This surge of motivation drives performance even higher. As the successes mount, workers begin to refine what works and what doesn't. Trial and error is replaced with streamlined processes that consistently produce even better results. As errors decrease and efficiencies grow, the performance curve shoots ever upward.

Feelings of confidence become rampant during the second half of Stage 4. In addition to feeling good about themselves, employees begin to express confidence in the new way of doing things. They even think better of the person who championed the change. Many of the early critics now take a form of begrudging pride in acknowledging they had misjudged the leader. "You've got to give her credit. She's smarter than I thought she was. She said it would work and, look, she made it happen."

Workers begin to tell others how well the new system is working. In fact, mature adults can become so giddy with each success that they act like schoolchildren coming home to show off art class masterpieces. They'll seek out the leader and eagerly tell him or her details of each new triumph.

The growing belief in the new approach spreads beyond the team that made it happen. Team members begin to proselytize and seek converts to the new approach.

Workers not only see how the change can help the organization but they also discover ways it can work for them personally. Individuals discover fringe benefits such as greater schedule flexibility, interesting new colleagues, more (or less) travel. And they learn that some of the things that irritated them about the old way are no longer a problem.

Stage 5: The Mountaintop

During Stages 2, 3, and 4, performance was below the level it was in Stage 1. Now, it's at last climbed to a height that matches the old way of doing things. The workers are now proficient in the new way of doing business. During this stage, performance continues to shoot upward as success piles upon success, errors are virtually eliminated, and costs are reduced. Change has been achieved!

As employees reach new heights, thoughts and feelings seem to blend:

"YES!"
"This is great."
"I love it."

The euphoria associated with mastery of a new challenge is one of the most satisfying emotions in all of life. Conquering the seemingly impossible produces feelings of exhilaration and joy.

Such achievements validate our beliefs in our own capacity to deal with challenges. "This old dog can still learn a few new tricks." In fact, employees can start to feel so good about themselves that they may begin to get delusions of grandeur. Perhaps it's the thin air at this high elevation! And what does a mountaineer look for after conquering the peak? A bigger mountain, of course.

"Why did I wait so long?" Each of us can remember a change we resisted despite the urging of friends and coworkers. Or we can recall reluctantly agreeing to sample a food we were convinced would taste terrible, only to discover it was delicious. Workers feel the same way when they find hidden advantages in the new way of doing things.

As a leader of change, you can expect that some of those who raised doubts back in Stage 1 now will be praising the change. You might even hear some of them say, "We should have done this years ago." Or the really irritating "I knew it would work all along." They may even claim it was their idea.

Tempting as it may be, don't self-righteously remind the resisters of their obstinacy or seek a pledge of future compliance to your requests. That's unlikely to do much good. "Failure is an orphan," an old saying goes, "but success has many fathers." It's just human nature for people to rewrite history in order to put themselves on the side of success.

The final surge in performance likely will be spurred in part by those who find innovative ways to apply the new approach. They'll invent new solutions to old problems. They'll devise applications no one has thought of. Their creativity will further fuel productivity, giving you added credence as a leader of vision who can harness the power of change. Concentrate on celebrating the people who made the largest contributions to the change rather than chastising those who lagged behind.

Chapter

2

PUTTING THE J CURVE TO WORK

Leaders and team members are often in different stages of the process of change. Management is usually in Stage 4 and heading into Stage 5 by the time they decide an idea is good enough for everyone. They've thought about it, discussed it at length, perhaps done a few pilot tests, and experienced the benefits before announcing the new corporate initiative. "Yes! We will consolidate the Purchasing Department into Finance. Imagine the cost savings, not to mention the improved efficiency!"

Meanwhile, the purchasing agents are about to face the emotional cliff. They see a radical switch in procedures and maybe a loss of status and pay.

The clock starts ticking as the reorganization is launched, and guess what happens to the leaders and to their followers? The leaders shoot up to the mountaintop anticipating massive savings and efficiencies. Meanwhile, most of the rank and file is heading south in Stage 2.

From their lofty peak, the leaders look down into that deep valley and think:

"What's wrong with these people?"
"These people don't get it."
"Don't they see the big picture and how important this is?"
"They lack the ability to do this."
"Maybe this just won't work in our culture."

The challenge is for leaders to learn to identify with the people who are resistant, understand their fears, and extend a hand to help them through Stages 2 and 3. Indeed, one of the greatest attributes of successful change agents is the ability to remember what it's like to be stuck on the cliff. It takes humility and courage to acknowledge that you, too, have been frightened and paralyzed. Doing so creates understanding and gives you compassion toward people who are resisting change.

You've probably seen interviews in the business press with much heralded business "innovators." Sometimes these hyperstrong executives will tell how a radical new idea came to them full-blown one morning and by the afternoon they were implementing it. That makes for a good story, but the more honest leaders will admit that everyone, including themselves, needs time to master a whole new way of doing business. Trial and error, they concede, is inseparable from change.

These savvy change leaders know how long it took them to get to Stage 5. They remember all the reading, discussion, coaching, and experimentation that preceded mastery. They have no delusion they can switch directions 180 degrees overnight.

Often, both resisters and leaders are, in a sense, stuck. Those resisting change are stuck in Stage 1, afraid to go off the emotional cliff, and many leaders get stuck on Stage 5's mountaintop, incapable of understanding the folks still back in Stage 1. Frustrated, these leaders talk to their followers like this:

"Just do it!"

"It's easy. I've done it hundreds of times."

"Come on. It will work. I promise."

"You'll like it once you get used to it."

Of course, in the face of their followers' fears, such words are meaningless.

The challenge for you as a leader or a coach, then, is to psychologically put yourself back at Stage 1 so you can empathize with those who remain stuck there. Try to recall a time when you resisted a change. A vivid memory of some of your own past resistance will help you understand in personal terms, not just platitudes, what they are experiencing. This capacity to recognize yourself in the other person's experience is the essence of the spiritual element in leadership.

You have good people working for you, and it just so happens at this time that they're stuck. They don't need time-worn phrases to inspire them to change; they need practical assistance, a safe environment, and sufficient time to learn. We all want to develop and improve. But we don't want to look like fools or lose our livelihoods in the process.

WHEN CHANGE GOES WELL

In its simplest form, the J Curve represents the natural history of change as it is lived out in both business and personal arenas. In other words, the pattern is the same whether we're adjusting to a new job or new culture, cooking a new dish, or adapting to a new home.

What happens after Stage 5? What will be the shape of the curve as time goes by? Will it simply keep on climbing? That's not likely. More commonly, performance begins to level out, and people begin to institutionalize the new approach. The excitement of the mountaintop fades into a sense of satisfaction with the new status quo. A new plateau develops. Then *what*?

It won't be long before another change will be proposed. The spark could be a competitor's actions, new regulations, or new opportunities. Whatever the instigation, you'll face another change, and the J Curve pattern will be repeated again and again.

When this sequence of J Curves is viewed from a distance, it begins to resemble a set of stairs, with each successive plateau of Stage 1 taking change higher and higher.

Ideally, then, performance will continue to improve through a series of plateaus and troughs as shown in Figure 2.1.

As the curve flattens and another steady state is achieved, the *new* way of doing things will become the *old* way. What was once resisted will become sanctified as *the* way we do things. Human nature seems to dispose us to become attached to the new way just as we did previously with the old way. Unfortunately, this also means that we will now probably resist changing from the new way of doing things to the even newer way.

There will always be some degree of resistance to the next major change. It's also true that the amount of resistance to the next change can be somewhat reduced by just having gone through a transition. How much it is reduced depends on many factors. Later, we'll explore some of the things that impact people's readiness and resistance to subsequent changes.

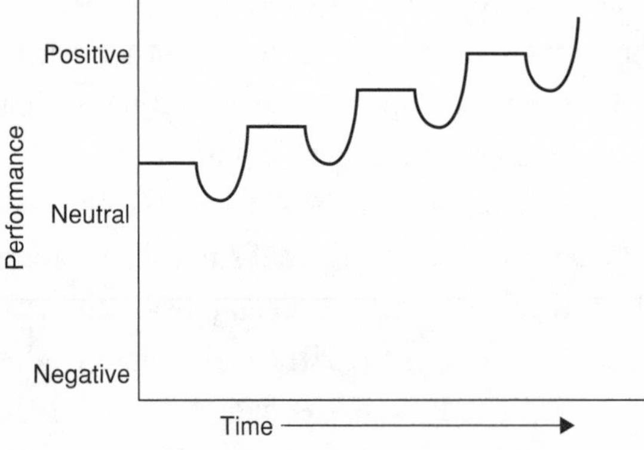

Figure 2.1 Continual improvement

Management gurus often advocate continuous rapid change. Even though some people can become accustomed to ongoing change (usually when it results in more money and advancement for themselves), there's a point of diminishing returns at which we all become exhausted and discouraged by the work involved in nonstop changes. In actuality, most of us need to spend some time on the new plateau rather than quickly rushing off the next cliff.

Leaders, especially the ones who haven't been directly involved in making a change happen, are often eager to launch something new immediately. But those doing the heavy lifting need time to consolidate what they've accomplished. They need to develop routines and shortcuts. They also may need time to catch up on all the work they had to put aside while they were coping with the last change. And they need time to decompress, slow down, rest, and socialize with coworkers. It's similar to a three-day weekend that allows you to take care of household chores, get more sleep, spend time doing hobbies, or just being with friends.

The practical lesson for leaders is this: allow workers to recoup before forcing them to move ahead with another big change. Let them savor how much they have accomplished before you tell them how much *more* they have to do. Even the boldest mountaineer pauses at the peak to savor the view. And if necessity requires another change, begin in a department or division that didn't have to lead the last change.

WHEN CHANGE GOES BADLY

The basic J Curve is like a Hollywood feel-good movie: good triumphs over evil, and everyone lives happily ever after. Life, of course, doesn't always follow that script. Some changes never climb to the dizzying heights of increased productivity and profitability. In the real world, the downward slide into the valley of Stage 3 may never end and, thus, Stage 4's ascent may not materialize.

Many reasons exist why changes don't produce the expected benefits. One reason may be that the idea wasn't a very good one. It may have been hastily conceived or just plain wrong. Research and planning are the best defenses against this kind of error. Knowing your industry, your company and, most importantly, knowing your customers are good defenses against foolish initiatives. Discussing the idea with a wide variety of people inside and outside your organization can also inject a strong dose of reality into your plans. Conducting small pilot experiments can help guard against sinking the entire enterprise.

Even with proper research and thoughtful analysis, good ideas may fail to yield good results. This usually occurs when the key leaders of change don't take into account the human dimensions of change. Encountering resistance, time delays, and escalating costs, many leaders panic and back away. When one idea isn't immediately successful, many leaders, and especially factions that opposed the idea, get interested in a different concept and then launch a new initiative. Instead of a series of J Curves with each stair step going higher, the partially completed Js keep going lower and lower as shown in Figure 2.2.

While not all changes will be successful, it is important to give a new initiative sufficient time and resources to get through Stage 3 and

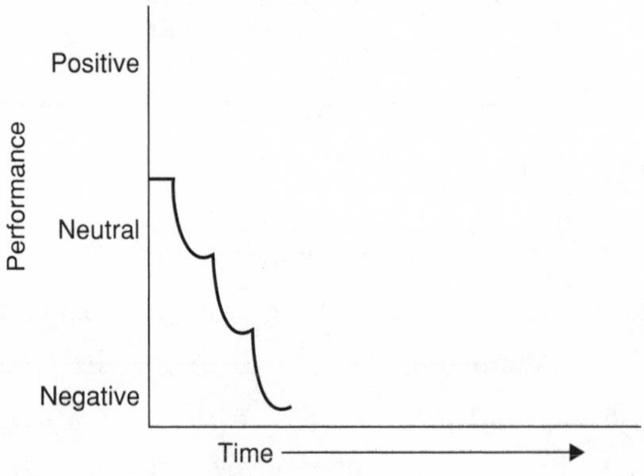

Figure 2.2 Successive drops

make the ascent up the mountain. Here's a handy tool that can help you avoid prematurely scuttling something that could prove to be very good.

We're all familiar with using benchmarks to measure improvement. Another kind of yardstick that's particularly useful in change situations is what I call a *negative benchmark.* It demarcates how low we're willing to let performance drop or how many resources we're willing to invest before we decide to discontinue the change.

It's akin to placing a stop-loss order on a stock. You might decide you're willing to keep the stock as long as its value doesn't fall below 20 percent of its current price. Once it drops that low, you will want to cut your losses and sell. Prudent gamblers also use a kind of negative benchmark when they carry a chunk of their money into the casino but leave the rest in their room hidden in a drawer. In essence, they're deciding how much they are willing to lose and setting a clear numeric limit.

The limits can be stated in terms of time and productivity. "If output doesn't exceed the current level within six weeks, then we'll have to revert to the old system." Or for losses you're willing to endure, you might say, "I'm willing to spend $25,000 on this pilot but not a penny more."

It's tough to know when to commit more resources to a change that is dropping down through Stages 2 and 3 and when to call it off. There are no pat answers. But one thing is clear: negative benchmarks should be established in Stage 1, before actually executing the change.

Leaders, like gamblers, are susceptible to the fallacy of thinking that a run of bad luck portends good luck on the next try. The leader who originated an idea is especially likely to fall into this trap. Just as a gambler may retrieve the money hidden in his room to wager a little more, many leaders decide to commit still more time, money, and worker-hours to ideas that will never work. Many "white knight" CEOs brought in from the outside to rescue corporations have stuck with their bad ideas until the board of directors finally replaced them with someone else.

When performance drops to the level of the negative benchmark, there are two basic options. One possibility is to simply abandon the new initiative entirely. Or the poor performance may trigger a dispassionate and comprehensive reevaluation of whether to commit more resources or to consider other alternatives.

Negative benchmarks can have the salutary effect of reducing conflict within a group that's split over which change initiative to endorse in the first place. Usually, two or more ideas compete, with each camp feeling its approach is correct and that the other idea will be a colossal mistake. The leader who begins to favor one proposal can break the deadlock by suggesting the establishment of negative benchmarks. The opposition fears that the failure of the change initiative could ruin the whole organization, or at least cripple it for a long time. With a negative benchmark established in advance, opponents have less reason to worry about the outcome. Because proponents are confident of the value of their idea, they're usually more than willing to agree to a negative benchmark to placate the opponents.

Of course, there is a potential problem with establishing and publicly announcing a negative benchmark. Opponents may try to figure out a way to scuttle the idea by interfering with its implementation. All they have to do is be less than enthusiastic in executing the idea and it may slowly sink to the bottom, triggering the negative benchmark.

To avoid such sabotage, a leader may decide not to publicly announce the negative benchmark. She may even swear the leadership team to secrecy so that the opponents don't know there is a lower limit.

A more forthright way is for the leader to candidly explain that the change is her idea and that she's willing to reevaluate it if performance falls below the negative benchmark. She can go on to explain that when the reevaluation occurs, there will basically be two possible interpretations. One is that the idea was deficient and it should be dropped. Or the idea is still good and some people weren't fully committed to its implementation. She can then say that her bias, because she believes in her idea, will probably be to try for another six months to make the idea a success.

The purpose of such a discussion is to explain to people that the best way to prove that the idea is bad would be for everyone to fully commit to making it work. The leader then promises that if they give 100 percent effort and results still fall below the negative benchmark, she'll be the first one to admit it was a bad idea and ought to be scrapped. Such a discussion may not eliminate all foot-dragging and resistance, but it can swing the energy of the group to give the idea a fair chance of success.

Aspiring pilots for high-performance jets are pushed to the limit to see how many gs (units of acceleration of gravity) they can tolerate. Business managers sometimes undergo a comparable test, but the question is *How many Js can you take*? Blood seldom comes from your ears, nor do you lapse into unconsciousness from too much change, but it can take a toll on your body.

Change is plural. Life's complexities often produce multiple changes simultaneously, with one J Curve layered upon another. Let's say you've moved to new facilities as part of the merger of two organizations. And as you're trying to adjust to new colleagues, a new reporting structure, a new boss, and new procedures, someone decides this would be the perfect time to convert to a new computer system. The stress of too much change in a short time can lead to burnout.

There's no magic number for how many major changes we can deal with simultaneously. That's because it's not just how many changes but also what J Curve stage you are in on each of those changes that determines the stress. Because the pressure is greatest in Stages 1, 2, and 3, you may feel overwhelmed launching more than one major change simultaneously. You might feel as though you are always behind and aren't in control of anything.

Multiple changes are more manageable if your progress is spread out across the full range of the J Curve. If, for example, you're entering

Stage 5 on one change and in Stage 2 on another, you'll likely be better able to handle the changes. While you may be struggling in the early stages of one change, your spirits could be soaring in another arena because there you're peaking.

Faced with change overload, most of us naturally adapt very sensibly. When it becomes impossible to keep up with everything, we prioritize (or take on our boss's priorities) and pick one change initiative on which to focus our energies. We push ahead with that priority while doing basic maintenance on the other change efforts. When the primary initiative reaches Stage 5, we select one of the initiatives that has been kept in a holding pattern and drive it forward. In essence, we avoid simultaneously being in Stages 1 and 2 on multiple changes.

Leaders could learn from this natural adaptation by not trying to drive too many changes all at once. When a leader takes over a business unit that's in trouble, for instance, there is a strong temptation to fix everything at once. You've probably seen a newly hired boss who literally walks around on day one with a clipboard taking notes of the changes he wants to make. The next day, or possibly the afternoon of the first day, he calls a meeting and announces all the things that are going to change.

In the long run, it's often wiser to let employees know that while many changes may ultimately be implemented, you're going to focus on one that is both important and achievable. When that first change has climbed through Stage 5, you can think about launching change in other domains.

Help Others through the Tough Times

Like gravity, resistance to change is a fact of life. And the range of resistance tactics is vast. If you think otherwise, try dealing with a child who doesn't want to go to bed or an octogenarian who doesn't want to give up his or her driver's license. We all prefer to keep doing things that are familiar to us because we know how to make them serve our interests. We resist changes that do not appear to be in our self-interest. The greater the perceived threat to our interests, the greater we will resist.

Resistance is greatest in Stages 1 and 2. In the workplace you can expect arguments, stonewalling, false promises, name calling, displays of anger, and diversionary tactics as people try to get you to stop making them change. Because we all tend to resist change, we should be better able to empathize with other people's fear and hesitance.

A major organizational change may be totally unacceptable to some individuals. This often occurs in mergers when reporting structures are changed, jobs are redesigned, and redundancies are eliminated. This means some people will be assigned to new positions which require significantly more work or a decrease in autonomy and status. They may find these changes so repellent that they decide to leave the organization rather than adapt to the new environment.

If people are going to leave rather than adapt, they usually do so in Stages 1 and 2. Here's a rough general rule about who leaves when: the best people leave in Stage 1, good employees leave in Stage 2, and poor performers never leave. The best people leave early because they have options. If they have serious reservations about a change, they can get another position easily by just saying "yes" to the headhunters who routinely call them.

When a top performer decides to quit because of an organizational change, it's often because no one took the time to explain the vital role and opportunities he or she will have in the new setup. Leaders become so consumed with bigger issues that they don't even take 15 minutes to tell each important performer how critical he or she will be to the success of the change. These few minutes of reassurance and discussion of specific opportunities can help guard against the loss of key players.

Absent any personal discussion, these high-performing individuals may feel they aren't appreciated and that they have diminished career opportunities in the organization. So they start looking elsewhere and you could lose them in a matter of days. Smart managers talk to their top people immediately, even before the announcement of the change, if possible.

Even if they have severe reservations, most good employees will try to accommodate to a major change through Stage 2. If their performance continues to fall, they too may begin to look elsewhere. In some cases, their opinion that they can't adjust to the new system may be accurate, and you will want to help them find a new position. With others, you can use the practical techniques described in this book to get them to persevere during the early phases of the change.

Low-performing individuals will tend to stay through Stage 2. They hope the change won't be successful, may drag their feet, and possibly try to sabotage the change to ensure a return to the old order. When they see that leadership is committed to the new approach, despite poor early results, these low performers may begin to talk about finding alternative employment. Help them find it. Don't make excuses for the new approach or offer false hope that they will adapt. Spend some time assisting them in making a transfer to another position within the organization that suits their style or assist them in securing outside employment.

A few individuals who were poor performers under the old system will be even worse in the new system. They won't leave voluntarily, and this may be the best time to work on developing their personal improvement plans and progressive discipline with termination as a possible outcome if they cannot adapt.

The concerns, complaints, and low morale of Stage 2 will be balanced by positive feelings as the J Curve turns upward in the second half of Stage 3. When the team rounds the bend and performance begins to climb, a palpable feeling of cohesiveness will develop. This jump in morale will be a welcome relief to leaders who have been trying to maintain the group's enthusiasm during the downward descent of Stage 2 and the long slog through Stage 3. The good news is that the motivational spurt will continue all the way to the top of the mountain.

As a leader your main responsibility comes in the first half of the J Curve. After that, your hardy band of true believers will begin taking more initiative to drive the change forward. Because they've experienced success with the new way, they can be highly effective at seeking converts among those who have been standing on the sidelines.

BUILDING ON CREATIVITY

All this talk about resistance and fear associated with change doesn't paint a flattering image of human beings. But one of our finest human attributes—our creativity—is released during the implementation process. Our resilience and adaptability comes to the fore when we have to deal with the challenges of implementation. Interestingly, this creativity takes a different form at each of the stages.

During Stage 2, the brilliant plan the leaders thought was going to produce a sudden victory doesn't seem to be working exactly as planned. At this stage, the creativity takes the form of the *generation* of ideas—it's a real-life version of brainstorming. Necessity is said to be the mother of invention, and frontline employees often have innovative solutions to stop the drop in Stage 2. At this point, wise leaders listen and learn from those actually doing the changing. These associates doing the actual implementation will volunteer, if asked, all kinds of ideas about how things could be improved. Not all of the ideas will be good, but one or two can make a big difference.

Often these novel ideas come from the most unlikely places. Young people, individuals who are new to the organization, and outsiders offer some of the most innovative ideas. The formal leaders need to step back and support the emergence of these new informal leaders and enable them to shape the direction and process of the change.

Sometimes so many ideas are offered that there's confusion about what to do. At that point a new form of creativity, called *crystallization*, is needed. One person takes two or three of the ideas that have been proposed and fashions them into a new solution. This synthesizes what was a confusing jumble into a coherent plan. Usually occurring during Stage 3, this new solution often prompts the J Curve to turn upward.

As performance climbs through Stage 4, the new way of doing things is working very well for particular customers, situations, or problems. Another form of creativity can expand these applications. Someone says, "You know, we could use this with our established customers as well as the new ones." Or "If we could waterproof this, people could use it at the beach or on boats." Or "If the night crew did this, too, we could double our output."

By encouraging such creativity during the middle stages, leaders can both speed up the process of change and improve its quality. Many managers falsely assume they alone are capable of coming up with innovative solutions. Tapping the intellectual capital of people at all levels of the organization gives team members an opportunity to shape their future as well as that of the organization. The joy people feel when they volunteer a helpful suggestion can buoy the spirits of the whole group during the dark middle passage. Like a proud parent, the leader feels great satisfaction in knowing that he created an environment in which everyone can participate in making the change happen.

HOW LONG WILL CHANGE TAKE?

Leaders and followers alike want to know "How long is this change going to take?" Unfortunately, no hard-and-fast rules exist for estimating how long it'll be before the J Curve runs its full course. As we'll discuss later, so many factors influence the time required for a change that it's often difficult to make a precise prediction.

However, you can calculate an approximate time by using your subjective judgment to answer three questions:

1. *What is your most optimistic estimate?* Let's say the shortest time in which you can imagine the change being complete is six months.
2. *What's your most pessimistic estimate?* This is your worst-case estimate, and thinking about a worst-case scenario you estimate 18 months.
3. *What's the most realistic estimate?* Imagine that your fair-minded estimate is 12 months.

Experience shows that the best quick-and-dirty prediction is about halfway between the pessimistic and the realistic estimates. Roughly 15 months in this example. You might refine the process by getting multiple people at different levels to respond to these questions and using all of their answers in making a calculation.

MAKE THE J CURVE WORK TO YOUR ADVANTAGE

Once you have a solid understanding of the J Curve, you can find many ways to put that knowledge to use. Here are a few of the ways you might use it.

Can you see how beneficial it would be for senior executives to teach the J Curve to middle managers, who teach supervisors, who teach front-line teams? When people understand the natural trajectory of change, they understand things are going to get worse before they get better. When they learn the common human reactions at each stage, they feel more comfortable acknowledging their own thoughts and feelings. As a result they have a greater sense of control and are more willing to move forward.

Perhaps the greatest benefit of teaching the J Curve to people is that the most important message gets communicated without words. People get the deep sense that the manager understands and cares. They feel more comfortable about the change because they know their manager doesn't expect them to perform miracles overnight. They feel they are being treated with respect because the manager is being honest about the challenges ahead.

Some leaders strongly object to the idea of publicly admitting that the change probably will go poorly at the beginning. They interpret this as negativity. Being positive and optimistic is all they want to focus on. Experience shows that honest explanation works better than denying the coming times of struggle and failure.

Everyone has gone through tough life changes—with their children, their parents, their job—and they know transitions are inherently difficult. If you ignore or gloss over the normal difficulties of Stages 2 and 3, people think they're being lied to or treated as though they were naïve and gullible.

You should always be upbeat as well as honest when you teach the J Curve. Tell them you know specific things they can do (you'll learn these techniques in this book) to speed the process of change and minimize how low performance will drop in Stages 2 and 3. Express confidence that the team will probably make the change happen faster than others expect. With your help they'll be able to transform the J Curve into a Nike swoosh or a check mark.

Teach up as well as down. The people above you will often have the most unrealistic ideas about how quickly the change can be implemented. Often it is your boss who needs to understand that the change she wants you to implement may take longer than she expects. Take time up front to review the J Curve with your superior and put some realistic and pessimistic estimates on how long the whole process may take. Creating this kind of mutual understanding reduces the likelihood that she'll blame you when her most optimistic dreams aren't coming true.

The Fog of Change

As with war, there's also a fog of change. Information is sporadic, and vivid stories of failure and success can distort your assessment of how things are going. Additionally, different groups at different sites move more quickly than others. And, a department that had been moving quickly ahead may hit a roadblock and get stalled or even regress.

The leader's bias is almost always to think the implementation is progressing faster than it really is. Leaders often focus on great successes in a few areas while disasters elsewhere may get ignored, leading to differing perceptions of reality. Who do you invite to stay in your office and tell you more? The person who brings you bad news or someone who has success stories to tell?

It's understandable why leaders err on the upside. They *want* to believe things are moving quickly. I remember being in a large regional engineering and manufacturing facility in a Fortune 100 firm that had undergone a mammoth merger. On the first anniversary of that change, the CEO went on closed-circuit television to announce to employees all over the world that "the merger is complete." The folks I was sitting with said, "Here in Phoenix it *isn't*."

Getting an accurate picture of how things are going can be hard. One way around this is to meet regularly—once every week or two—and let people tell you how things are going in their area of responsibility. To do this, it's often useful to demarcate change with a more precise scale. Expand the simple 1-2-3-4-5 stages into tens, 21-22-23, etc., and 31-32-33, etc. This creates room for people to provide more refined estimates. It's crucial that you make sure people understand they won't be punished for honestly telling you their true assessment of how much or how little progress has been made. This is the time to know what's really going on, not what you'd like to believe is happening.

Determining Where Everybody Is

People start at different points along the J Curve. Most may be at Stage 1, but a few will be scattered through the other four stages. Sensitive leaders recognize these individual differences and tailor their assistance to the needs of each person. Those in Stages 1 and 2 require intensive coaching and encouragement, while those at Stages 4 and 5 can be enlisted to help with that coaching.

To determine someone's exact stage, pay special attention to thoughts and feelings as well as performance. Be careful not to rush to judgment when listening to what people say. Asked how his group is doing on an implementation, a manager might say, "Oh, fine. Yeah, we're working to make it happen and we feel good about it." Based on that, you might think his group is somewhere in Stage 4.

Probing more deeply, you'll often hear a different story. "Well, actually we're just getting started and we've run into some real problems. I've got some worries about how much work it's going to take and whether we'll ever make it work. But don't worry, we'll get there one way or another."

What do you think now? Based on this more complete answer, it sounds as though they're just starting Stage 2. The first answer is what the other person thinks you want to hear. But if you show you sincerely want to know by asking more detailed questions, you'll get a more realistic description.

Managers at all levels usually need training in how to make people feel comfortable expressing their fears and concerns. One of the critical skills is to resist trying to counterargue or immediately address negative comments. The goal is to get people talking so that they've been able to tell you what they're really thinking and feeling. Remember, people's initial comments usually don't tell the whole story. Even after people have voiced their doubts and concerns, the manager doesn't have to provide solutions. Another approach is to ask the group how they'd recommend dealing with each of the issues that has been raised. You'll be amazed at how clever and constructive many people will be. They'll often come up with solutions that are better than the ones you were considering.

Variations on the J Curve

Although change usually follows the J Curve pattern, there are some variations. The most common exception is what I call the "honeymoon curve." Immediately upon launch, things go extremely well. Performance is up, not down, and most people are feeling very good about the new way of doing business. Hold on. Don't celebrate too quickly. That initial success may be followed by a drop that will then conform to the more normal J pattern. This honeymoon curve can occur when management pours a lot of resources into preparing and educating people for change. Things are going so well after a month that management moves on to other concerns and that's when the wheels come off. Suddenly problems occur and the teams get discouraged.

The key here is making sure that management stays involved until the curve is moving up into Stage 5. The education and resources are great, but nothing is as important as management's continued involvement with the day-to-day progress of the change.

You may see a similar honeymoon pattern when you analyze the profitability of an organizational merger. Profits can climb initially because costs are cut. But after this initial burst, the organization faces the greater challenge of adding dollars to the top line of the income statement. When this reality hits, the typical plunge associated with Stage 2 can be even more severe. It is the responsibility of leaders at all levels to manage the entire process of a change.

A hockey stick curve is the hope of most managers. This means performance begins to climb at the launch and just keeps going up. Several conditions can produce this outcome. A heavy investment of resources in preparation and education plus management's continued involvement is one of the best strategies for obtaining these results.

Sometimes you'll also see the much-dreamed-of hockey stick curve if the change entails only a slight adjustment to the old way of doing things. This is one of the major advantages of making small changes.

Because this book focuses on larger changes that involve more radical shifts, a drop in Stages 2 and 3 is to be expected. It's these more substantive changes that cause people to hesitate and resist.

Immediate and continuous improvement also occurs in situations in which people have been operating under truly ineffective leaders or a completely dysfunctional management system. For instance, the removal of an oppressive boss may send workers' performance soaring, and it may just keep rising. In actuality, this usually only happens when performance was very high in the distant past *before* Attila arrived. His presence suppressed output, and his removal is a second change that allows people to bounce back up to their previous levels.

A comparable situation may occur when a large corporation purchases a successful small company. When Mega Inc. imposes its management systems, profitability at the small firm falls apart. If the next change involves allowing the small company to return to its original operating systems, profitability may dramatically recover.

THREE REALITIES OF THE J CURVE

"The true test of a first-rate mind is the ability to hold two contradictory ideas at the same time and still function," according to North American writer F. Scott Fitzgerald. With slight modifications this observation can be applied to the implementation of change. The true test of a first-rate leader is the ability to hold three contradictory realities in mind at the same time and still move forward.

First, the leader must be imbued with the benefits of being in Stage 5. You must be confident that the change will produce wonderful results and must remain confident the organization can successfully complete the change.

Second, the leader must always be aware that change is a process and that people will have to go through the many stages of the J Curve before success is achieved. You must plan for each of these stages and not be disappointed when setbacks occur.

Third, as the leader you must be able to mentally put yourself in Stage 1. Doing so enables you to better understand people's doubts and resistance. Remembering your own instances of resistance can be a real help. You'll be better able to empathize with people so that you can sincerely help them go over the emotional cliff and deal with the frustrations of Stages 2 and 3.

That's a lot to keep in mind. By moving between these three realities, you can be a part of, yet remain above, the daily ups and downs of the change process. With the tools described in Section 2, you will be astounded how well and how quickly people can scale the seemingly impossible mountain of change.

Chapter

3

INFLUENCING PEOPLE TO CHANGE

You stand on the cusp of a great new endeavor, bursting with confidence that your ideas for changing this operation are exactly what are needed. Being chosen to lead this change is a great opportunity to help the organization and to make your mark as someone who can get things done. Filled with excitement, you're eager to see your team's reaction to the brilliant, innovative plan you're about to describe to them.

Let's stop the action for a moment to locate yourself and your team on the J Curve. All of you are approaching the metaphoric emotional cliff. But where are your eyes focused? You're probably consumed with images of what it will be like at the top of the mountain. Profits will rise, costs will plummet, customer satisfaction will soar, and you'll be lauded as the leader who made it all happen.

However, while you're beguiled by the heights, where is most of your team focusing its attention? As your eyes go up, theirs go down. And when they look over that emotional cliff, what do they see? It's not a Yellow Brick Road. Instead, they see pain, suffering, and hard work—the "monsters." Instead of seeing the low-hanging fruit on the tree at the top of the mountain, they picture all the thorny underbrush and boulders they'll have to surmount to get there.

Leaders focus on the future and all the benefits that are going to flow to them and the organization. The rank and file locks onto the present, focusing on the costs rather than the rewards of change. Instead of thinking of the organization, workers are concerned about how it will impact them.

A comparable gap involves how leaders and followers perceive the magnitude of the change. Regardless of how big the change looks to the leader, it looks larger to those whose lives are most impacted by it. For instance, let's say a planning group is reviewing the firm's use of space. It discovers the four-person market research unit is on the west side of the building on the fourth floor, while the marketing department is on the east side of the third floor. It takes only a few minutes for the planners to decide to move the market researchers down to the third floor next to their colleagues. This has the added advantage of freeing space on the fourth floor to accommodate accounting's desperate need to expand.

In the context of all the decisions the planning group has to make, this is a relatively minor one. But what's the effect on those four people in market research? Enormous. Being moved to the east side means they will park in the lot rather than in the structure where their cars are protected. And now they have a long walk to the cafeteria because it's on the fourth floor, west side naturally. Add to all this that they'd made friends with their former neighbors in accounting, and now they'll seldom see those people.

It's similar to ice skaters joining hands to form a whip. For the skater at the center, it takes merely a small action, involving only a second or two, to turn 90 degrees. But the effect of that slight alteration in course is magnified as it progresses along the line until the skater at the far end is whipped forward at high speed through a long arc. That's what change can feel like to people on the receiving end down inside the organization.

These differences between the leader's and follower's perceptions of the change show up in many ways. Take a guess who thinks the change will happen quickly and who knows it's going to take a long time? Leaders usually underestimate how long the change will take and followers overestimate the time required. What about perceptions of how much work will be involved?" Again the leaders usually underestimate and the followers guess high—perhaps because they know they're going to have to do most of the work.

Leaders often are oblivious to this radical disparity in perspective and that leads to communication and reception problems. Messages from the top down are ignored, distorted, and viewed with extreme skepticism by people on the front lines. They see the leaders as out of touch with reality and not really understanding what it's like down in the trenches. Conversely, when the rank and file tries to communicate problems upward, their messages of concern often are viewed as whining.

Let's go back to you, the leader, and the team in Stage 1 prior to the announcement of the new initiative. What is the most common way we try to influence people to change? Whether directed at one person or at thousands of employees, our first efforts at inducing change usually involve communication. In fact, it's often communicate, communicate, communicate. This can include one-on-one talks with key individuals, multiple speeches, video presentations, or newsletter articles to reach an entire organization. Each form of communication has the goal of informing people in order to gain their support. By explaining the rational basis for the change, we hope to help people understand the value and importance of adopting the new approach.

The communication may take the form of presenting all the facts of the situation. Laying out all the pros and cons is usually called education, and it's designed to let people draw their own conclusions about the necessity of change. The expectation is that they'll reach the same conclusion as the leader about what needs to be done. In practice, the communicator uses persuasion rather than education by stressing the information that favors his conclusion and glossing over inconsistent information. Whether persuasion or education, the logic of all communication is straightforward: give people information to change their minds and you'll change their behavior. Let's see how well that works when the audience is filled with skeptics.

YE OLD GENERIC CHANGE SPEECH

You've surely heard it more times than you care to remember and may have given it yourself a few times. When applied to a major change, such as a significant shift in business strategy or adopting a new process, the communication emphasizes the same outline of key points, though not always in the inflated language of the following example. Here's the outline for the speech.

THE GENERIC CHANGE SPEECH

The Vision
Necessity of Change
Irrevocable Commitment
The Plan
Promise of Support
Expression of Confidence

The Vision

In the beginning is the vision, and the vision is good. The leader vividly portrays the mountaintop and the wonders we'll behold when we get there: higher profits, improved efficiency, and happy workers everywhere. The virtues of this corporate Eden are described in glowing phrases, regardless of whether any of the leaders have ever actually been to this shining city on the hill. They've probably only received a postcard from a consultant who claims to have made the trip many times.

Imbued with their vision, many leaders speculate about the possibilities of additional mountaintops that will come into view once this peak is achieved. "We'll expand customer access to 24 hours a day, plus we'll give a guaranteed one-day delivery. Next, we'll go after the China market with over three billion consumers, and that will put us in a position to buy out our major competitor." Leaders think this kind of blue-sky vision will be inspirational; in truth, it adds to followers' trepidation.

Anticipating that many followers will be wondering why there is a need to change when things are going fairly well, the speaker lays out the reasons.

The Necessity

The leader lists the many forces that make change imperative. This list is remarkably similar across all industries and bears a striking resemblance to the reasons given in stories featured in this month's issue of any major business magazine. The prime suspect: competition.

The leader explains the new competitive forces operating in the marketplace. Someone has found a way to do things better and cheaper, while delivering more quickly. But the competition isn't just coming from one source, it's sprouting up everywhere. Major players in other industries have suddenly discovered our little market niche, and they're coming after it with bigger bucks and more efficient systems. To make matters worse, the competition isn't just domestic anymore. It's global.

Although stated here in hyperbolic language, it is true that competition is reshaping our current business environment. To give a sense of urgency to the message, the speaker may drop the names of defunct Fortune 500 companies, victims of a failure to change. On a more positive note, he mentions some highly successful companies with a reputation for innovation. In this histrionic version of the speech, the message is *Change or die*.

Technology, too, is driving the change. The speaker explains that just to maintain our current market position, we must incorporate these technological advances. To leapfrog the competition, we must innovate. Rapid advances in technology require that we adopt cutting-edge concepts, and most of them come with no guarantee of success.

In addition, shareholders are demanding short-term results. The ruthless, relentless denizens of Wall Street are incapable of seeing beyond the next quarter's results. What this means for us, the speaker says, is constant innovation to keep the key numbers and ratios marching upward. Remember, he adds, these shareholders have other investment options and they could sink our stock and our options in a flash. We may dislike it, he adds, but this is another fact of modern business life we must accept.

If these factors weren't enough, our customers are insisting that we change. Customer loyalty is a quaint relic of the past. It would be a relief if they were crying "What have you done for me lately?" But the new refrain is "What are you going to do for me now and in the future?" Consumers want more and more at lower cost.

Whether the list of market forces is longer or shorter, the message is clear. There's not just a wolf at the door, there's a whole pack of wolves in the boardroom salivating in our face. Change is an economic necessity. Our survival—*and* your job—depend on it.

The Commitment

The speaker's voice softens with sincerity as he acknowledges that it won't be easy getting there. There will be challenges.` Old ideas, old processes, and old habits may block our way, but we're irrevocably committed to moving ahead. As his passion and volume increase, we're told to give up any thoughts of returning to the old ways because there's no going back to the past. We're going to burn the bridges to our old patterns of doing business. We must move forward.

The Plan

Then there's another shift in tone as the speaker describes *the* rational solution to all our problems. It's a bold plan that will take us directly from the plateau of Stage 1 to the mountaintop of ultimate success. How many of these plans have you seen? Every freshly installed leader, no matter how large or small his or her sphere of influence, seems to feel a deep, almost biological imperative to create a new strategic plan.

After working more than 20 years on the challenges of managing change, I've developed a rule for judging these plans. It's called the "Glitz Rule," and it states: "The better the quality of the graphics, the more problems we're going to have." Anytime you see more than five colors in a slide in the PowerPoint presentation and the boxes in the flow chart magically move through space, you know you're in for real problems. Dazzling slide shows can look and sound good on the first run-through. But when you actually try to use the plan as a road map for implementing change, you realize the details are sparse and incomplete. Sometimes you turn a page expecting to see the phrase "and then a miracle happens." And of course the "S" word—synergy—is sprinkled throughout. Now the speech is starting to build toward the close.

The Promise of Support

After reviewing the key points of the plan, it's time to discuss how we're going to achieve our goal and who will be doing it. Naturally it's going to be a "team effort." Everyone will be involved. Upper management did its part by working long and hard to develop the plan; now it's up to the middle and lower ranks to make it happen. Of course, upper management proclaims they'll remain supportive of the worker bees.

Perhaps this is too cruel a characterization. But most of the heavy lifting invariably is done by those further down the pyramid. One of the key lessons we've been taught about the strategy of execution is that senior executives must remain involved with the actual implementation. In any event, after the promise of support, we come to the big motivational sendoff.

The Grand Finale

The final line in the speech is almost always the same. It starts with the phrase "I have confidence that..." Do you know how it ends? There are two concluding variations. Usually the final phrase is "*you* can do it." Sometimes the pronoun is different as in "*we* can do it." Even when "*we*" is used, old hands suspect the real meaning is "*you.*"

If the boss has a dramatic flair, the grand finale may be accompanied by the theme from *Rocky* as well as the handing out of T-shirts and baseball caps emblazoned with the slogan of the new order.

Regardless of the size of the audience or the amount of hoopla, everyone from the highest CEO to the most humble team leader relies on this basic communication format to persuade people to accept the change. We're often told that change requires that we communicate, communicate, communicate. Therefore, the speech is repeated over and over with the hope that one of the iterations will work its magic. Does it?

REACTIONS TO PERSUASION

There are good reasons to give that kind of launch speech, and yet how effective is it in actually changing people's behavior? Metaphorically speaking, does it get skeptics to go over the emotional cliff? Audience members tend to fall into one of three broad patterns. Although the percentage of people in each may vary slightly from situation to situation, the following three groupings invariably emerge.

Ready to Where

These people are enthusiastic, buying into the leader's vision of the future and willing to follow his or her leadership. They'll gladly serve on the task force and they'll volunteer themselves and their work groups as beta sites for new pilot initiatives. Thank goodness these people exist! Without them, no change would even get started, let alone be successfully completed.

They're called the Ready to Where people, because they'll go in any direction the leader takes them. In a play on words, you might also say they're like ready-to-wear clothing; they require no tailoring. The fit is so perfect you can immediately walk out the door with it.

Wait and See

These folks applaud politely after the speech, smile, may even shake the leader's hand, and say "You can count on me." But when they get back to their work area, how do they do things? The same way they always have. As these supervisors and managers go back and relay the proposed change to their work groups, they may pay lip service to the new vision but everyone gets the unspoken message: This too shall pass and the less we do, the faster it will disappear. For appearance's sake, these individuals may make a halfhearted attempt at the new approach. But they'll execute it in such a way as to virtually guarantee failure. At least they can then say they tried and it didn't work.

Resisters

These are the vocal opponents, and they're not always polite about it. They're loud, they argue, get emotional, make threats, and openly oppose the change. They're convinced you're going to lead them off a cliff from which there is no return and they're not going to go quietly. Many of their arguments may be unfounded or illogical. Their real goal is often to simply protect their own self-interest. Even so, it's worth paying attention to them. Some of their points and suggestions may be valid and can be usefully incorporated into the change.

ATTENTION INVERSION

Of these three groups, which gets the most attention from managers? Typically, it's the Resisters. It roughly parallels the 80/20 rule in which 80 percent of management's attention is devoted to the people who resist change and only 20 percent goes to the supporters.

Why do we focus so much of our time and energy on those who are resisting? Often you can't avoid them, so naturally they get your attention. They adamantly raise objections in public meetings or corner you in private with their vociferous disagreements. Their continued dissension raises the scary thought that they could convert some of your supporters and completely undermine the change initiative. It feels as though you must address their arguments. Also, because you know your idea is so reasonable, you're convinced you can persuade anyone of its merits.

Some objections are well reasoned and deserve to be understood and incorporated. Therefore, you need to seriously devote some of your attention—maybe 20 percent, but not 80 percent—to their reasons for criticizing the change. You should ask them for constructive suggestions on how they would modify the initiative. Unfortunately, no clear rules exist for distinguishing "reasonable" from "resistance." You must use your best judgment.

Not all Resisters are created equal. When people who play a key role in the organization raise objections, obviously you need to spend more time with them. Even there you must place time limits. Being key players doesn't make them immune to getting caught in emotion-based resistance. Of course, they'll never see their arguments as emotional or self-serving.

In an attempt at fair-mindedness, we often fall into the trap of treating all objections as though they were purely rational. When our first attempt to convince doesn't succeed, most of us try again and again. The Resisters and the Wait and See people can lure you into this ongoing dialogue by dangling tempting bait in front of you. "I can see where you're going with this. Part of me agrees with you, but I'm not quite there yet." Your hope is engaged, and you believe that if you can eradicate their tiny lingering doubts, you can get them to switch to your side. In rare cases, that may work and so it's worth trying once or twice. However, too often, you'll never marshal enough evidence. Each new thing you suggest only causes them to raise more objections.

For instance, let's say you want to organize the finance department into teams. First, you go to the leadership group with evidence of how well teams have worked in other companies. Their reaction is, "Our corporate culture is different." You try to blunt this argument by explaining how the Mid-Atlantic states division of this very corporation is using it successfully. Their response: "Yes, but this isn't the Mid-Atlantic region." In the face of their objections, the only proof that will convince them is that it works on a local basis. So, you collaborate with a friend who manages purchasing to set up a pilot project of teaming in his department. Three months later, the numbers and morale are looking great. Armed with these statistics from their own backyard, you go back to Finance. What do they say this time? "Yes, but that's Purchasing. We're different."

It's not just people in Finance. Evidence that the new approach works for other people seldom convinces those in the Wait and See and Resister categories.

What are these people waiting for? Some of those in the Wait and See group are watching to determine if you're really committed to the change. They're waiting to see if the Resisters will wear you down. Perhaps you'll become enchanted by another idea and forget this one. There could be a crisis of such severity that all new initiatives are put on hold. You may even be replaced! Any of these outcomes means these people who are hanging back won't have to change. They're not going to jump on the bandwagon until they're sure the wheels are moving forward and they have evidence that it's going to carry them to the Promised Land. These employees want to see how the change will affect their self-interest.

What, they ask themselves, will be the impact of this change on my career, salary, and everyday work life? For all of us, WIFM (What's in it for me?) is the default position from the moment the generic change speech begins. While the leader talks in global generalities, workers are translating the big words into local specifics. Given their self-focus, the people with doubts are not convinced by learning how much the company will benefit or how well similar efforts have worked in another division. They're waiting to see whether the change benefits or harms their personal interests.

By waiting, they also get to avoid the heavy lifting as well as the risks and costs of going first. If the new reality looks as though it will last, they'll then begin to search for ways to make it work to their benefit. Will they be able to ensure all the privileges and benefits they currently have under the new arrangement? Can they use it to improve their current and future career, advancement, and compensation? Who will they be reporting to and will they be able to work with the new person? What will their new duties be? Until they actually see people like themselves experiencing benefits of the new approach, they'll stay the present course rather than change.

THE IMPORTANCE OF FOCUS

So what can you as leader do? The single most important guiding concept is Focus. Begin by focusing "80 percent" of your attention on the Ready to Where individuals who are eager to change. This may be a small nucleus. However, they're ready, so help them get the project started.

Then get this select group to focus on only one initiative. Picking one may be hard because there is so much you need to do and all of it seems important. Most likely you can't do it all at once. Trying to do it all at once will actually slow the implementation process. It's better to pick one place to begin. In deciding which aspect of the change plan to focus on, you often debate between one that promises a big payoff and one that is sure of success. Try for balance and favor the one of which you are most certain. Early successes motivate those already on board and simultaneously quiet some of the Resisters.

Next, it's time to focus even more by selecting one project within the one new initiative. Then focus on the first phase of that project. Now get even more focused by defining the specific actions that individuals will need to take at the beginning of the first phase of the project. Once those small steps have been determined, let them go at it. You know from the J Curve that their first steps will probably meet with failure, and you can prepare yourself and this team for the chorus of "I told you so's" from the self-righteous naysayers sitting on the sidelines.

After the initial missteps, successes will begin to accumulate as the change goes through the normal J Curve process. As the change progresses, you'll be presented with opportunities to involve more people. Don't fall back into the trap of thinking you can now recruit all of the holdouts. Keep focused, and identify one or two of the key Wait and See people or departments you think you could now convert. As you slowly gather one ally after another, they will become advocates who recruit still more people. Even some of the Resisters who had reasonable doubts will join the endeavor and may go on to be your most vocal champions. Often, there are a few Resisters who will be unyielding. When you decide that it's not worth the effort to try to crack these blocks of granite, find ways to help them locate a different setting in which they can work more comfortably.

The 3Ps of focus are people, project, and particulars. Focus on the enthusiasts, focus on one specific project, and focus on the details of the concrete actions that need to be taken first. Too often, managers expect people to know what to do and don't take time to help them clarify these first steps. Chapter 5 addresses this important skill of how to break down the change into simple ground-level steps.

DOES PERSUASION CHANGE BEHAVIOR?

Talking to people and trying to persuade them is the primary communication tool we use to induce change. Yet how effective is it? This question is especially important given that we're interested in changing what people *do*, not just what they *say* they're going to do, what they *want* to do, or what they *think* might be a good idea to do. We want to change behavior, not just attitudes and intentions, and we're often faced with people who are committed to continuing to do things the way they always have.

Let's use the three patterns of reaction to the change speech as a starting point for this analysis of the effectiveness of communication in getting people to change what they are doing. Clearly, the Resisters weren't changed by the speech. They'll continue to act and conduct business as they always have. That's roughly a third of the audience that remains unmoved.

What about the Wait and See folks? They smile and nod like bobblehead dolls but continue to do things in their time-honored pattern. You may have changed their attitudes but not their actions. That means you've got two sizeable groups that have not been effectively persuaded. What about the remaining segment?

Following your speech, the Ready to Where people have embraced the change and they're actually living it. If we could attribute this group's shift in behavior to our persuasion, then it still would have been worthwhile to have given the speech. Don't jump to this conclusion hastily. More thoughtful analysis raises doubts about whether our communication was primarily responsible for this group's enthusiastic support of the proposed change.

Some individuals in the Ready to Where segment were probably presold on the proposed changes. They have probably been dropping hints for months, hoping the boss would adopt this course, and others have secretly been doing it the "new" way for quite some time. Other people have bought in to the boss's new approach simply because she is the boss. If she explains why the company needs to change direction and head west, this group would salute briskly and start changing course. She could come in the next day and announce that north was actually the direction to go and these employees would immediately start marching to that pole while complimenting her on her agile strategic thinking.

Many people just want to please the boss because their jobs and futures depend on gaining the leader's acceptance. So when she says, "change," they do. They care more about *what* the leader wants than *why* she wants it. Regardless of the logic or the direction, they will happily agree.

So when you really analyze it, persuasion is not very effective in changing the *actions* of people who are committed to their current way of doing things. The Resisters are unchanged, the Wait and See people are unmoved, and only a small fraction of the Ready to Where group actually changes its behavior as a result of understanding the logic and validity of the communication. This conclusion runs counter to our commonly held belief. We are repeatedly told that communication is the critical tool for getting people to accept change. Then again, the conclusion may not be that surprising if you think about how hard it is to break a personal bad habit, even when you're really persuaded that you should change.

Limitations of Persuasion

Why is the highly vaunted communication tool of persuasion so weak in the face of emotion-based hesitance to change? To answer this question, consider the president of a midsized company who wants to take the business forward to new heights. He presents a bold plan to commit the company 100 percent to e-commerce, instead of the staged approach it has been using. After his announcement speech, imagine we could conduct a confidential survey of the employees' views about going completely electronic. Let's say that on the key question, opinions can range from 1 (strongly disagree—"Let's go back to the pretechnology days") to 5 (moderately agree—"I'll do it, but I really like things the way they are") to 10 (strongly agree—"Eliminate the sales force and sell the bricks and mortar").

Steve, a sensible middle manager, circles scale point number 6 indicating slight agreement. Asked why, he replies, "I firmly believe Internet commerce will be the most important part of our marketing and sales ten years from now. But we can't jeopardize our existing sales and delivery channels in the process of making the transition. We need to use caution in moving forward."

While we may be forced to circle only one number on the scale, we're flexible enough to circle any of several numbers. There are usually a range of attitude positions we'd be comfortable with. Steve, for example, circled the number 6 but he'd be willing to go as high as 7 on the scale and he'd be okay going down to 4.

As illustrated in Figure 3.1, Steve's latitude of acceptance goes from 4 to 7. In practice, this might mean that he'd support a proposal to move forward with one limited pilot project (7). Or, more cautiously, he would volunteer to serve on a task force that would conduct a six-month analysis of going 100 percent electronic (5).

Outside this range of acceptable positions are sets of positions that will be rejected. In the case of Steve, he rejects the range of positions from 1 to 3 and 8 to 10 on the attitude scale. Steve would reject anything as conservative as cutting the e-commerce budget by 25 percent and would resist anything as risky as signing off on a plan to immediately transfer several major product lines to electronic commerce.

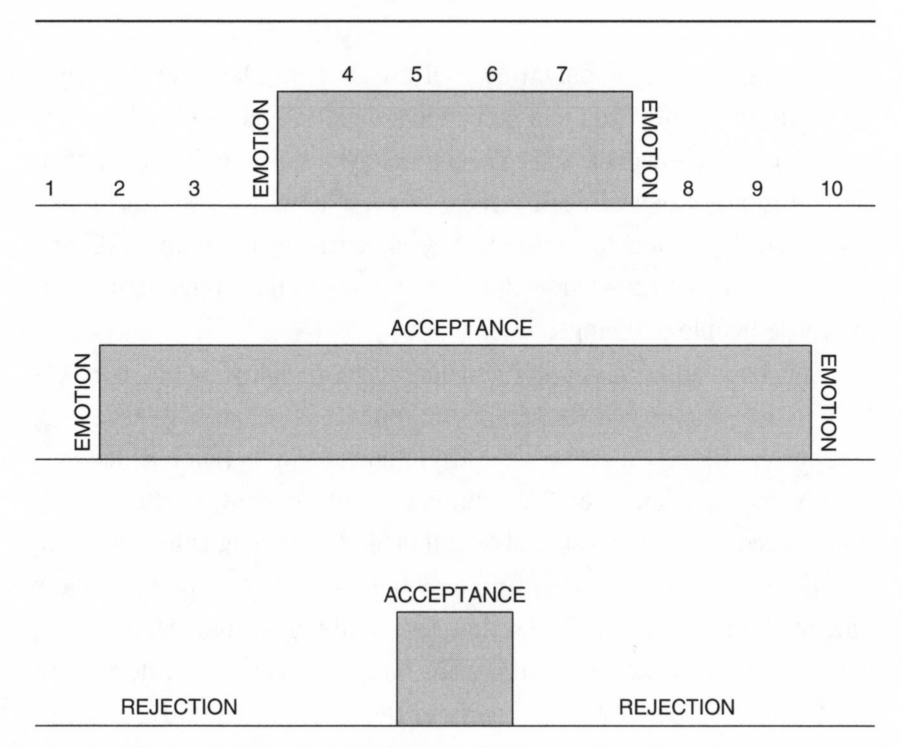

Figure 3.1 Latitude of acceptance

Here is the key point: persuasion will be effective in changing someone's attitude position within his or her range or latitude of acceptance. The boss could talk Steve up to a 7. And his recalcitrant work mates could convince him to go down as low as 4. However, no amount of persuasion will get Steve to accept the positions in the ranges that he currently rejects.

In this example, the boundaries between 3 and 4 as well as between 7 and 8 are emotional barriers demarcating the limits of what is acceptable to him. Crossing them is comparable to going over the emotional cliff on the J Curve. Because persuasion typically only addresses the mental, or cognitive, aspect of what we believe and do, it isn't effective in overcoming the emotional blockages to major change.

Persuasion, education, and similar communications should be the influence tools we turn to first, and we must be realistic about their limitations. Persuasion only works within a person's latitude of acceptance. Stated bluntly, you can convince people to endorse an idea they already generally accept. You're very unlikely to talk people into an idea they presently reject. Because most of the changes we want to make involve getting people to do things they currently reject—after all, that's why they're resisting—persuasion is not going to be enough in itself to get these people to change.

Now let's factor in another consideration. In everyday life, our latitude of acceptance can vary from one topic to another: wide on some, narrow on others. On issues that are important to us (such as how we do our job), our latitude of acceptance is very narrow. Because of its importance, we are emotionally committed to keeping things just the way they are and essentially find only one position acceptable. That's narrow. Conversely, on things that are relatively unimportant to us, we'd be willing to accept a very wide range of positions. "I don't care what color you paint the stairwells in the parking structure. You can leave them as is, or paint them puce; it doesn't matter to me."

This leads to the key question: does the change you're implementing affect things that are important or unimportant to people. If it's a major change, it will most likely impact things that are very important to people: their jobs, income, career, work responsibilities, etc. Therefore, on these significant changes, persuasion is going to be of little practical value.

This is a startling conclusion given the way communication is touted as crucial. We shouldn't generalize too broadly because these communications can change people's thinking and may help to allay their general fears about the change. But persuasion is a weak tool for getting Resisters to change what they are actually doing.

Despite its limitations in changing behavior, we're tempted to use persuasion to influence people because it promises to be relatively quick and it is respectful of the other person. It definitely is the first approach that should be tried, and tried several times. But what do we do when persuasion doesn't work? We started out trying to be reasonable but after two or three attempts to persuade, we switch to a more powerful mode of influence.

Coercion: The Wrong Alternative

Too often managers resort to force. Frustrated with the failure of repeatedly trying to persuade people to change, they make threats. Out of the pressing need to get the change initiative implemented, they turn to giving an order or issuing an ultimatum. "The time for talk is over. Here's what we're going to do and if you want to keep your job, you'd better do it." Or, "I'm the boss. That's why you need to do what I say."

Threats work, at least in the short run. But they spell disaster over the long haul. Coercion temporarily quiets the voices of resistance and can get people to act as though they're going along with the change. But the minute the manager isn't there to monitor how they're doing things, employees go back to the old way.

Threats can change behavior; however, they don't change attitudes or feelings. When coercion is the manager's primary tactic, employees change their behavior in order to avoid punishment, not to experience the benefits that come with doing things the new way. While they act differently, people still don't like the new way of doing things.

Coercion has an addictive downside. Because coercion tactics do get immediate results, many managers come to rely on threats. Essentially, they're being reinforced for using them. If there's resistance to the next change, these managers will usually resort to even greater levels of threat.

If all that weren't bad enough, threats also create feelings of resentment and anger. Workers retain the memory of how they were mistreated and humiliated, and they remember who did it to them. It's said that revenge is a dish that is best served cold, and employees will wait for the chance to get even. They may do it by gradually and subtly withdrawing their support of the change. They may deliberately sabotage it. Or they may discretely hint about their boss's weaknesses to her boss.

Let's summarize this discussion of common influence techniques. Managers should start with education and persuasion, and if that changes people's behavior it's a quick low-cost solution. These communications may influence a few attitudes but virtually no behavior changes. You don't want to be a coercive tyrant, but what is the alternative? You need a way to constructively and respectfully get people to change what they are doing.

Given the major drawbacks of both persuasion and coercion, managers have been searching for a middle way that they can use to overcome people's resistance and more quickly implement organizational changes. The search is over. The new method is called activation and it's described in Chapter 4.

Chapter

ACTIVATION: THE ART OF TURNING RESISTERS INTO DOERS

You drive up to the car dealership reminding yourself of your budget constraints. All you want is a reliable car for commuting purposes, nothing expensive or fancy. That's what you tell the salesperson too. And he quickly confirms that the lot contains a wide selection of trustworthy, low-priced models that will be great for commuting. He points to where the economy cars are parked and suggests you head over that way while he gets keys to some of the vehicles.

As you begin walking, a new sports car catches your eye. It's all black (your favorite car color), and you decide to check it out. It looks even better up close. Running your hand over the body confirms the sleekness of its lines and the quality of the workmanship, and then you notice the subtle highlights in the black paint.

Still, you repeat your mantra "I will stay within my budget. All I want is a reliable car for commuting." Then the salesman approaches with a ring of keys and says, "Doesn't our new entry-level sports car look great? Take a peek inside." As he opens the door, you inhale that great new-car fragrance mixed with the aroma of leather seats. It's so enticing you can't help but climb inside. Wisely the salesman says nothing and stands back to give you some private time to notice, touch, and smell the car's many features. At the salesman's urging, you turn the ignition and hear the powerful sound of the engine.

"It's great to see someone who can really appreciate the details of a stylish sports car that's also reliable and economical," he says. "But the only way to get a true sense of this baby is to drive it. Why don't we just go around the block so you can at least say you've driven this magnificent machine? Then we can come back and look at a more conventional choice."

Right. Come back and look at the economy models. After you've felt the power and handling of the sports car and heard the quality of its sound system, your mind won't be on your mantra. Instead, you'll be figuring out if you can skip lunch three days a week to cover the higher monthly payment of this car you absolutely must have.

How did this happen? You didn't want to purchase a sports car. How would you have reacted if the salesman had suggested that you first look at the more expensive car before the lower-priced models? Most of us would bristle and resist any attempt to get us to look at anything but the budget models.

Somehow, in a matter of minutes, your attitude has changed. It happened through a process that has been widely used for centuries but has never been clearly specified or named. I call it *activation*. When this natural process is bolstered with some good management practices and applied to people, activation can work wonders in converting Resisters into doers and believers.

ELEMENTS OF ACTIVATION

Let's begin by identifying the key aspects of activation. Most of these elements are a part of the naturally occurring changes described in the sports car example. Others will need to be added to make activation a management tool you can use to speed the process of change in the workplace. Once we've established the basics, we'll look at why and how activation is so effective with people who are resistant to change.

Break the Change Down into Small Steps

Your goal may be a complete transformation but the most effective way to make it happen is through tiny progressive steps. Remember your conversion at the auto dealership? You're not going to buy a sports car; you'll simply look in the window. You're not going to buy a sports car, merely sit inside. You're not going to buy a sports car, just take it around the block. You're going to buy a sports car.

Front-load Rewards

This means giving praise and other rewards in the early stages when the going is tough and employees are grappling with their darkest fears. You experience the rewards of the new-car aroma and the pleasure of its handling and acceleration.

Make It Safe to Make Mistakes

When facing change, our imaginations run wild as we picture the humiliation of publicly revealing our incompetence. In the car example, once you're sure you're not obligated to buy the car, what's the harm in slipping behind the wheel to see how it feels?

Provide Guidance and Training

Learning to do a new task gives you knowledge and a sense of control. Change is much less frightening if you've learned how to deal with it. Even though you don't have to learn how to drive the car, many organizational changes do necessarily include an educational component.

Encourage Involvement

If you get to define exactly what small steps to take in implementing a new venture, you have a sense of ownership about the new way of doing things. Extrapolating this to the auto example, you'll be more willing to take the car on a test drive if you can determine the route, the speed, and the maneuvers you can attempt.

Sympathize with Negative Feelings

When we bemoan our fate as we drop off the emotional cliff, we want someone who understands our negative feelings. The car salesman may say, "Yes, this is different than what you planned to buy. And it's true this may be a little more than what you were hoping to pay." Of course then he'll probably add, "But you're not the kind of guy who has to stick by a plan if a better option presents itself. You're not afraid to change your mind when it's the sensible thing to do."

Make It Easy to Get Started

The path of change can be greased by making it simple to take the first few steps. After all, it costs you nothing to take the sports car around the block.

Stay Committed to Implementing the Change

In a business environment, the leader has to remain involved during all five stages of the change process. He can't simply delegate. It's his responsibility to see the change through to a successful conclusion.

When used in combination, these elements of activation provide a practical way for you to help those with doubts and fears go over the emotional cliff and continue through the challenges of Stages 2 and 3. When the J Curve begins to rise through Stage 4, you can back away and let the natural process of activation spur the individual to greater heights.

HOW DOES ACTIVATION WORK?

Imagine you're famished as you enter the grocery store. You approach a woman dressed in white and standing beside an electric skillet. She smiles and asks, "Have you tried our new garlic rosemary tofu sausage?" You're firmly on record with family and friends as not liking tofu so you're ready to reject the object on the toothpick being extended toward you. On the other hand, you love garlic and rosemary bread; plus, you didn't have lunch today.

Reluctantly, you take a small bite. Not bad, you think, taking an even bigger bite. Not bad at all. The texture is unusual, but the taste is very nice. As the hostess turns to offer a sample to another customer, you take your toothpick and stab a bigger piece before she turns around.

How did you go from virtually hating something and resisting it to actually sneaking more of it? This is activation in action. It relies on the old adage: Try it, you'll like it. Activation is designed to get you to like it by promoting early positive experiences so that the J Curve of change becomes shaped more like a check mark: the person quickly moves from resistance to conversion.

Amazing things happen to employees—and ultimately, to whole organizations—if you can get them to honestly start doing things the new way. Activation provides the techniques that will help workers get started through the scary parts of change so that they can experience its rewards. As they taste success, they'll discover for themselves how to make the new way work to their advantage. When they see how it can serve their interests, they'll come to believe in it and like it.

Activation is a bottom-up approach to change. It gets employees to take actions in the new direction even though they have doubts and fears about doing so. Persuasion, by contrast, is a top-down model. Persuasion assumes you have to change employees' attitudes before they'll start to actually move in the new direction. In a sense, activation begins with the feet, while persuasion starts with the head. Activation uses behavior to change hearts and minds, while persuasion attempts to change minds in the hope that hearts and actions will follow.

The elements of activation are designed to get people started in the new direction and to sustain them as they go through the frustrations and setbacks of Stages 2 and 3. Then, as performance improves in Stage 4, people actually begin to experience the pleasures of doing things the new way. "Hey, this is quicker." "Wow, this makes my job easier." "This new software makes it possible to do all those things I always wanted to do." At that point their attitudes and feelings change and come into alignment with the new approach you've been implementing.

It is the *direct personal experience* of the benefits that produces the change in thoughts and feelings. No speech, regardless of how well written or delivered, can have the impact of actually experiencing the benefits for yourself. And the sooner the individual experiences success by doing things the new way, the faster the attitudes and feelings will change.

This has a surprising implication for the occasions when it is most important for managers to use persuasion. Interestingly, during Stage 4 a leader's persuasive message can have much more impact than in

Stage 1. By the end of Stage 4, employees are beginning to like the new way of doing things and are open to listening to the logic behind the new approach. At this point, they've gone past their fears and they now understand how the new process actually works. People are finally in a position to understand the linkages between what they are doing and the leader's larger strategic objectives.

Producing major change in a business organization usually requires a radical transformation. But such a dramatic change isn't going to happen overnight. Fully implementing a change means making lots and lots of small changes in order to produce the total transformation. Activation is based on the assumption that incremental change is a part of every major transformation.

Businesspeople and psychologists have long been aware that you can change people's attitudes by first changing their behavior. Until now, no one has forged that insight into a comprehensive set of tools that can be consistently used to implement changes in the workplace. By systematically using the elements of activation, you can lead individuals and whole organizations through radical changes. The details of how you can put each element of activation to work for you will be described in detail in the subsequent chapters.

WHY DOES IT WORK?

Persuasion is directed at thoughts and beliefs while activation works because it addresses people's feelings. It provides the means of neutralizing the emotional barriers that block employees from acting outside their latitude of acceptance. Even though activation tackles the underlying emotions, it doesn't require managers to become junior psychologists or get all touchy-feely. Instead, it's a simple and straightforward approach that any manager can use to help people adopt a new way of doing things even though they may have personal doubts about the change.

Activation is based on the idea that when workers say they don't like a change, it is largely their fear talking. They're like shy 8th-grade boys at a school dance. A part of them is silently wishing to be a part of the fun, but another part of them is afraid of the shame associated with appearing incompetent and not wanting to fail. The immediate cost outweighs the possible reward. So, for now, they opt out.

Let's look at how each of the elements of activation tackles the negative emotions that cause employees to resist change. Activation reduces the sources of employees' fear, and it supplants negative feelings with positive ones. As a result, they're willing to start acting in ways they would normally resist, and soon their attitudes and feelings align with their new action patterns.

It's easy to see that a small step in the new direction is much less frightening than a complete transformation. A total shift in the way you do your job or in your managerial style can be scary because it evokes images of all kinds of monsters lurking over that emotional cliff. "Will I be able to do this?" employees ask. While they may have doubts about their ability to climb the whole mountain of change, they know they can take a step or two in the new direction.

Making employees feel safe about making mistakes is aimed at another major source of fear: "What happens if I fail? Will people laugh at me? Will I lose my job?" Knowing that nothing bad will happen frees employees to experiment with the new approach. If they can trust the boss when he says that making mistakes is part of the learning process, they'll be emboldened to attempt things they've never done on their own.

Because people are very likely to be successful in taking small steps, you'll have reasons to praise them and front-load rewards. Even if they aren't initially successful, you'll want to recognize them for trying and encourage them to try several more times. These rewards up front serve to neutralize the negativity of the employees' fear with a positive feeling of well-being.

When employees receive training in how to successfully do things the new way, their confidence grows as they gain an appreciation of exactly what is going to happen and what they should do. Developing an understanding of exactly how to implement the change helps create a feeling of being in control that banishes fears of incompetence and ignorance.

In the same way, being involved in determining exactly how the change will be implemented gives employees an added sense of control. Usually the ideas employees suggest are ones they feel certain they can do successfully, so they feel more confident. Plus, their suggestions almost always involve ways of tackling the change that will result in benefits to them. For example, they may recommend ideas that will require less work or that will enable them to be even more successful. This leads to even more positive feelings that further reduce their uncertainty and fears.

When we're hesitant to do something new, we view even the slightest obstacle as a major barrier and use it as an excuse not to change. These little annoyances make change feel burdensome and oppressive. Watch how quickly negative thoughts enter your consciousness when you seriously consider all the work involved in starting a project that you've been postponing for weeks or months (e.g., doing annual performance appraisals or cleaning your office). Making it easy for people to take the first steps clears away these obstacles and the negative feelings that go with them.

HOW DOES ACTIVATION WORK IN PRACTICE?

A regional accounting firm's business revenues had been decreasing over the past three years. During this period the managing partner frequently urged employees at all levels to do more business development. He stressed the importance of bringing in new clients and expanding the services used by existing ones. Despite his repeated pleas and heartfelt words of encouragement, virtually no new clients were acquired and business continued to decline.

When persuasion didn't work he resorted to blatant threats. "If revenues continue to fall at this rate, we're going to have to start letting people go. None of us want that so you've got to bring in more business." The threats produced more anger and depression than revenue. Not surprisingly, a new leader was appointed.

Ella, the new managing partner, developed a plan to change the culture of this staid accounting practice. Her goal was to make the firm's culture, in her words, more entrepreneurial. After describing her vision in general terms, Ella switched from the lofty language of planning and strategy to the concrete words of implementation.

A decision was made to focus on changing the behavior of the younger accountants rather than the more senior partners who were already tapped out as rainmakers. These younger people did most of the actual work on accounts; however, they weren't accustomed to doing business development. Many of them, in fact, were more comfortable with numbers than people, and the idea of building relationships to bring in more contracts was both foreign and frightening to them.

Realizing she'd have to rely on the senior members of the staff to fully implement the change, Ella began by teaching them the activation approach. As part of this training of the senior staff, she got them involved in spelling out concrete things they could do to coach and encourage the younger staff members.

The training of the junior staff began by helping them break the concept of "business development" down into easily doable baby steps. Instead of talking about "schmoozing" clients, Ella asked each of the younger staff associates to refine one brief story they could relay in their next face-to-face meeting with an existing client. People made up their own personal tale to tell to their client, and it always involved a project that the firm had recently successfully completed. This was a relatively painless request, and everyone agreed to do it. Much to Ella's surprise and pleasure, just having the junior staff talk to clients about recent successes actually generated some new business. The new contracts were small, but they got people's attention and made them realize this new business wouldn't have come through the door if employees hadn't told their stories.

As a next ground-level step, the junior associates were encouraged to follow the story with simple questions such as "Do you think we could help you with a project like this?" Or "Are there any similar financial projects that we might help you with?" This time the results were much more significant and occurred more quickly. It became clear to everyone that simply asking how they could help the client resulted in additional contracts. More and more steps followed on the road to getting people to start doing "business development," and they involved simple progressive actions the junior staff could easily take. In addition to breaking the change down into ground-level steps, Ella used several of the other elements of activation.

Prior to any meeting between any junior staffers and a client, a senior manager met with each of the younger staff members to coach them on the stories they would tell. As the individual repeatedly practiced the story, the senior manager front-loaded rewards by repeatedly praising each new telling of the tale. They also explicitly told the junior staffers that this was a rehearsal session and that it was all right to make mistakes. They were primed to explain that making mistakes was a necessary part of the learning and improvement process.

The junior staffers were encouraged to shape and plan the story so that they felt comfortable with the wording and flow. Through this process of creating and polishing their own stories, they became more involved in making it interesting and effective.

When a junior person expressed fears and doubts about telling the story or directly asking a client for more business, they received a sympathetic response. The senior managers were trained to acknowledge that it could be frightening and that doing anything new raised doubts and uncertainty. These managers were explicitly told not to react authoritatively to these expressions of negative emotions. Specifically, they were *not* to say anything such as, "This is part of the job, and you better get used to it." Or, "It's only going to get worse, because from here on out generating business is going to be a bigger and bigger part of your job." Or, "This is nothing. Let me tell you how much harder it was when I was in your position."

When the junior person returned from each client meeting, the senior partner made it a point to inquire how things had gone. Even when the storytelling hadn't gone very well for a particular staff member or the questions didn't produce more business, the manager praised the staffer for beginning the process of telling a story and asking questions. Major successes were greeted with general office recognition, and the standard was slowly raised for everyone.

Because the managers stayed involved as the junior people went through the J Curve process of learning how to begin doing "business development," everyone felt they were part of the change. The junior people didn't feel they were alone, and they knew someone was available to help and coach them. The senior people began to take pride in their success at helping the young people grow and develop.

HOW DO YOU MOTIVATE EMPLOYEES TO CHANGE?

In contrast to persuasion, which assumes individuals listen to communications and make their own internal decision about whether to change, activation relies on external incentives and rewards. This means activation has important implications for the topic of motivation.

"If people don't want to change, you can't make them change." This idea is popular among people who don't want to change and among managers who have failed to get their employees to change. It gained credence decades ago when psychotherapists put all the responsibility for change onto the client. If the hours of talk didn't produce results, clearly it was the patient's fault. Of course, the therapists charged for their own services even though they supposedly weren't responsible for the lack of progress.

In the business world, this belief was translated to mean there was little a manager could do to get people to change. At best, some leaders were supposedly blessed with the magic of charisma that mysteriously inspired employees to want to change. Or managers used special skills of persuasion so that workers became motivated to change.

You can find abundant evidence in your own life to refute the idea that people won't do something unless they want to. We all do things we don't want to do: pay taxes, clean the bathroom, visit relatives we don't like, and spend endless hours in airplanes. The list goes on and on. In fact the "you have to want to change" belief is contradicted on a daily basis. We don't want to wake up at an early hour, put on uncomfortable business clothes, change our diet to healthy food, have a long commute, or sit in committee meetings either. But we do so nonetheless.

The adherents of the "have to want to change" belief often defend their position by asserting, "Yes, but you wanted to get a paycheck, so really you did want to commute to work." No, that bit of rhetoric alters the nature and level of the question. While it is true that I do want to earn money, I still don't want to endure an hour of tedious travel twice a day to get it.

Activation provides the conceptual understanding and practical steps to help people change, even when they don't think they want to. How can managers use this to their advantage? Almost always, people change because of the possibility of future benefits. You change vendors because the new one will save you money and provide better service. You switch your allegiance from the old boss to the new one because she'll give you more responsibility and include you in the decision-making process.

People change their behavior if there are sufficient incentives for doing so. In economic language, we are willing to pay the cost of change if the rewards make it profitable. This reasoning suggests that if you give employees sufficiently large rewards they'll do most anything. While that may be true theoretically, it needs some practical qualification.

It can be expensive to dangle all those carrots. We'd like to get people to make changes without having to spend an arm and a leg. Providing tangible rewards could turn out to be very costly. So managers seek a balance point where they provide enough incentives to get people to do things the new way but not so many rewards that it breaks the budget.

Sometimes even when you dangle a lot of rewards, employees still won't change. The promised benefits may not be large enough or they may not be the kinds of rewards people really value (e.g., toward the end of tax season an accountant would rather have a vacation day than the fee associated with still another tax return). Incentives may also be ineffective because the person won't get them until far in the future (e.g., "You'll get something extra in your paycheck at the end of the year. I promise.") Or it's uncertain that they'll ever actually receive the rewards in the distant future.

Activation capitalizes on these practical insights about incentives by front-loading small low-cost rewards that are inexpensive for you—the manager—and that are easy to obtain and are tailored to the needs of the employee.

MOTIVATION: INTRINSIC OR EXTRINSIC

Activation has implications for another important idea about motivation. "Are employees motivated from internal psychological sources or external rewards?" Many people say they do their work for the pure pleasure of doing it ("I love my work"). Comparisons are made to play and recreational activities in which the incentives to perform are the intrinsically pleasurable feelings of doing the action. By contrast, extrinsically motivated people do their jobs to obtain external rewards, such as money, career advancement, and social recognition.

Most managers like to think of themselves as intrinsically motivated, and they regard lower-level employees as externally motivated. This self-perception is linked to a more general negative attitude toward extrinsic motivation that is fairly pervasive in our society. For example, you should do well simply because it's a good thing to do, not just because it has a pecuniary benefit. According to one psychological interpretation, giving extrinsic rewards to people who are intrinsically motivated will actually decrease their motivation to perform.

Putting aside the discussion of the merits of intrinsic versus extrinsic motivation, there is another question that is seldom, if ever, addressed: "How do people become intrinsically motivated to do their work?" Financial analysts may have inherited mathematical abilities, but they have to learn how to enjoy applying their abilities to doing hours of accounting. Similarly, the natural salesman may have loved talking to people since childhood; however, he has to learn how to use that talent so he can experience the pleasure of making sales.

The idea here is that people have to learn to become intrinsically motivated to do many of the things that give them pleasure. If there is learning involved, then it implies that the person had to go through a J Curve process. At what stage did the person become intrinsically motivated to do things the new way? The answer is that it takes until Stages 4 and 5 for people to begin to find the benefits associated with the new approach.

How do employees get to Stages 4 and 5? A few may have had immediate success, but most received extrinsic rewards during the hard times of Stages 2 and 3. These early rewards enable them to persist so that they discover the rewards inherent in the new way. Employees who don't get these early rewards give up when they fail in the early stages of a change. They drop by the wayside and never experience the rewards the new way of doing things can produce. In sum, extrinsic rewards help people persist down the new track until they experience the benefits that are inherent in the new approach. It is the experience of the rewards that are inherent in the new way of doing things that then produces the feelings of intrinsic pleasure and motivation.

Organizational change, like individual change, requires extrinsic rewards in the early stages to keep employees going until they experience the rewards that are an inherent result of the new approach. When employees personally experience these benefits in Stage 4, their attitudes and feelings change so that they become intrinsically motivated. The front-loaded extrinsic rewards that managers introduce are a crucial element in getting employees to a place where they are intrinsically motivated to do things the new way.

WHEN SHOULD YOU USE ACTIVATION?

Each of the major influence techniques has advantages and disadvantages. Understanding these pros and cons can help you decide which one you want to use when.

Persuasion

The primary advantage of persuasion is that it's relatively quick and easy. At best, it only requires a few minutes of talking. Persuasion can be effective in changing employees' behavior as long as the new position is inside their latitude of acceptance.

Although a leader's kick-off speech for a new initiative probably won't produce much behavior change, it can reassure doubters that at least there's a coherent plan, even if they disagree with it. The speech may not convert the resisters into active supporters of the change; however, it can reduce the overall level of fear in the group. This reduction in negative emotions can be very helpful when activation is then used in conjunction with persuasion.

Persuasion can be effective in changing attitudes, but it is much less effective in changing behavior. This is especially true when you are trying to get employees to take actions that are outside their latitude of acceptance. Because it doesn't produce much behavior change, managers are forced to keep repeating their persuasive message in the hope that it will get employees to change. This repetition is time-consuming and frustrating.

All in all, persuasion is most effective with employees who already basically agree with the new direction. It's important to make certain these employees understand the rationale behind the change. Repeating the reasons for the change and linking it to larger organizational strategy can also be very useful in Stages 4 and 5. At this point in the change process, people are much more receptive to understanding the logic of the change.

Coercion

Coercion's big advantage as an influence technique is that it works and it works quickly. Even though it changes behavior in the short run, it doesn't change attitudes or feelings.

Employees will begin doing things they would otherwise resist, but they'll only keep doing them as long as the threat of punishment remains. Once the threat is gone, they'll regress to the old ways of doing things. The use of coercion has several other major disadvantages. When employees comply with the threats, the manager gets reinforced for using coercion and is more likely to do it in the future. Also, employees who were subjected to threats will be primed to retaliate and resist future changes. This means the cycle of threat and retaliation will continue and probably escalate.

Coercion should only be used in crisis situations in which immediate action is absolutely necessary. It's critical not to persist with coercion.

Once the crisis is past, the manager should stop making threats and return to the use of persuasion and activation to keep people moving forward.

Activation

The outstanding advantage of activation is that it changes attitudes, feelings, and behavior. It just does so in reverse order. The main disadvantage is that it takes a little more time than persuasion. Fortunately, this extra effort only occurs in the first half of the J Curve because once the curve starts to ascend, the manager can let the natural process take over.

Since communicating the reasons for a change can shift some attitudes, it's best to begin with persuasion. However, if several attempts to persuade haven't produced sufficient behavior change, it's time to switch influence tactics and now use activation with the key resisters to get them to take action.

For most managers who use activation techniques to influence people, rather than persuasion or coercion, there is still a learning process that will take time and has its own J Curve. Fortunately, activation tools and skills can be mastered quickly. Once mastered, activation is usually much faster than repeatedly trying to persuade people to change.

The elements of activation aren't that complicated, but managers need the same kind of detailed guidance and front-loaded rewards to help them learn to use this new approach. In essence, you can use activation to help managers begin to use activation with their employees. The next chapters provide a detailed road map on how to begin the process.

SECTION

2

EXPANDING YOUR CHANGE TOOLBOX: ACTIVATION

Chapter

5

COMMUNICATE AT GROUND LEVEL

Prior to the launch of a lean manufacturing initiative, Graeme has many things to think about. For starters, there's the big picture. Graeme knows how this change fits into the logic of the organization's strategic initiatives for the year. To increase share price, the company must increase profits. One sure way to do that is to reduce production costs. And the most effective way to do that is to implement lean manufacturing.

Graeme is also thinking about how he'll coordinate the initiative with the multiple departments and managers that are involved. He must consider the politics and personalities of each, so that a turf battle doesn't sink the whole initiative. Third, he must keep within his overall budget. Fourth, he's projecting out six, twelve, and even twenty-four months to manage future phases of the initiative. And if all that weren't enough, Graeme is worrying about how to manage his boss and how to deliver any bad news that may come up in Stage 2.

With so many things to keep in mind, Graeme, like all good managers, has become skilled at thinking in abstract terms (e.g., reassigning human and hard resources, creating synergies, horizontal and vertical integration, value propositions, and integrating the supply chain). The strategy and planning phases of a change initiative require this kind of abstract thinking and language. So, understandably, managers use generalities, jargon, and acronyms as shorthand for all of the factors they need to take into account.

The day of the big announcement and the lean manufacturing kick-off meeting arrives. Graeme wants to say something inspirational. He reminds everyone of the organization's glorious past and calls upon their *love and dedication*. Graeme talks about the need for *commitment to the corporation* and *perseverance toward the new initiative*. Next, he gets personal by speaking about his hope that they will be *open-minded* about the initiative and have a *positive attitude*. Graeme then reviews some of the new skills they'll have to develop: *multitasking, time management, communication with teams and across functions,* and *emotional intelligence.* He mentions how they'll have to *be flexible,* be willing to think *outside the box*, and invent new ways *to work smarter, not harder*.

As he concludes, Graeme returns to the theme of *love for the organization*. He extols the workers' *loyalty* to the company. And in the final lines, he says he fervently believes in their *ability to work together as a team* and that when they do work together *they will achieve greatness*.

Graeme brilliantly delivers the speech and indeed many people leave the meeting feeling inspired. Unfortunately, it's unlikely to really help people come to grips with the emotions that are blocking the resisters from actively implementing the new initiative. The prime reason: his speech is peppered with the language of a strategist and a planner. The key words (italicized above) are abstract and don't really address the concrete changes people will actually have to make. Frontline people especially, and even middle managers, are concerned about exactly what they are expected to do and to achieve.

High-level words are great for strategy and planning but not for implementation. Effective leaders are able to step out of the strategist-planner role and get into the practical implementer role. Communicating exactly what changes people need to make is a crucial element of making this switch.

Because implementing change involves *actual behavior*, it requires words that describe what to do down at ground level. Implementation is not really about *being committed, persevering, being open-minded, having a positive attitude, thinking outside the box, multitasking*, or any of those other platitudinous phrases. It's about actually getting people to act differently. Implementation requires leaders to use a different mindset and a different terminology.

The first critical tool in the activation toolbox is to break the change down into doable steps. By communicating at ground level, you let people know exactly what they can do to begin moving in the direction of the change goal. Using simple words to describe first steps reduces people's resistance to the change and makes it much easier for them to get started.

Beginning to use ground-level language represents a big personal change for most managers. In truth, we like talking in generalities and we do it a lot. Abstract terms don't put many demands on us or on our listeners. We think we know what we're saying and they think they understand. Because everything is so high level, each person attaches his or her own meanings to the generalities.

General descriptions also have the apparent advantage of avoiding conflicts that might arise if we discussed details. While everyone can agree that the new initiative will require *commitment*, disputes can arise when it turns out that commitment means that we're going to have to work the next three Saturdays or that the only existing employee break room is going to be converted into a storage area.

God and the devil are both said to reside in the details—and so does change. That's where reality is. Implementation comes down to getting individuals to do things differently in the details of their everyday work lives. The specific sacrifices those details entail is what creates resistance and conflict. Sensing the objections that might be raised if they say too much, many managers seek to avoid arguments by staying up in the clouds.

That's enough of persuading you of the benefits of talking at ground level. Activation is all about behavior so it's time for some ground-level definitions, examples, and practical tools you can put to work to activate change.

USE YOUR ALTIMETER

During the implementation phase of change, you want to switch your language to describe the change in plain concrete words. A good way to understand ground-level communication is by using an altitude metaphor to define how far off the ground our language is from earthly realities.

40,000 Feet: Global Generalities

This is the land of the unfettered generality. When used to describe organizational goals, common 40,000-foot words include *innovation, excellence, quality, leadership,* and *customer service.* When we append additional adjectives such as "*world-class...*," we go to even greater heights.

This is the domain of mission statements, visions, and broad strategies. And these are the right kinds of words for communicating such general goals and values. Our job as implementers of change is to take those high-level words and bring them down to ground level.

Too often, when describing how people can change to achieve these lofty objectives, we continue to talk up at 40,000 feet. We say someone should be *proactive, flexible, creative, visionary,* and *a team player*. Again, these are fine starting points. But to actually help an employee understand the exact actions he needs to take in going over the emotional cliff, we must talk in terms of specific behaviors.

30,000 Feet: Psychological Processes

This is the realm of psychological language, so statements about values, beliefs, emotions, motivation, and personality attributes fit here. For instance, when you describe someone as having a *negative attitude* and wanting him or her to be positive, you're at the 30,000-foot level. We're operating at this psychological level when we complain that people must *understand* the need to change, because you're really talking about the beliefs and thoughts inside their heads. Similarly, talking about *having passion* and *needing to care* about the customers is the language of emotion. Saying someone *lacks a sense of urgency* is commenting on his motivation. We're using 30,000-foot words when we say the *introverts* need to be more *extroverted,* that the *analytic* people need to be more *intuitive,* and that we need people with a more *entrepreneurial mindset*.

If all you're doing is describing someone, this psychological language is an acceptable starting point. If you sincerely want to help employees change how they act, you have to talk in much more specific terms.

20,000 Feet: Broad Patterns of Behavior

Now we're finally talking about behavior, but we're doing it in general terms. Examples here include saying that people need to *improve their people skills* and *communication practices*. Or that they should *learn how to sell*. While these are all worthy goals, they don't provide realistic directions for individuals and companies trying to change.

10,000 Feet: Focused Behavior Patterns

At this level, instead of asking someone to "improve people skills," you might urge managers to *recognize outstanding performers*. "Communicating better" could be sharpened to *keep people updated on the project*. And "learning to sell" might become *develop your knowledge of the company's products and services*. Getting this low represents real progress from that blue-sky verbiage, but we can be even more specific.

Ground Level: Specific Behaviors or Outcomes

Saying something positive to each member of the team once a week is an example of a ground-level description of "recognizing outstanding performers." In the same way, sending everyone a weekly e-mail that discusses goals achieved, problems encountered, assistance being sought, and objectives for the next week is more specific than "keeping people updated." "Learning about the company's products" could mean taking an hour this week to read the sales materials for one product line and giving a five-minute summary at our Monday staff meeting.

You can practice your skill at recognizing language altitude by carefully listening to people's statements about change goals. This is especially easy to do in planning meetings, where so much of the language is in the stratosphere. At this stage of developing your skill, it's fine to start by learning to recognize high-level words when other people use them.

It's interesting to see which types of people seem most at home with 40,000-foot terms. The tendency to talk at high levels seems to be positively correlated with (1) intelligence, (2) verbal ability, and (3) position in the organization. Put another way, it's those at the highest levels of the organization who have the greatest addiction to high-level words.

There are good reasons why senior managers use this kind of language. Their responsibility is to develop broad strategies and to make large-scale plans. Problems occur when executives keep using the same language to talk about how goals and strategies are going to be achieved.

Avoid Holding Patterns

It's okay to begin with the high-level words. But we must avoid getting stuck up there. Have you ever heard a manager say something like "These people need to be more motivated. They've got to really care about this. We want them to be committed and give it their all. This is no place for slackers. At a crucial time like this we all have to put our nose to the grindstone." What do you hear? Be motivated? Really care? Be committed? Give it their all? Nose to the grindstone?

Essentially, this manager has just opened his thesaurus and is using one synonym after another. He thinks he's communicating and being more specific, yet all he's really doing is circling in a high-level holding pattern. That's not going to help people change. He needs to find ways to get his language down to the level of action.

Ground-level language is the most crucial element of using the activation technique to produce change. When you use high-level language to describe change, you're talking up at the mountaintop of Stage 5. High-level words actually create fear. "Am I really capable of thinking outside the box?" "I'm an engineer, not a psychologist. I'm not even sure of my own emotions, let alone having the emotional intelligence to sense what's going on with other people." To reduce people's fear of taking the first few steps over the emotional cliff, we need to be very precise and concrete about what they should do. Activation is based on getting people to move forward to take action, and we use ground-level language—not blue-sky words—to specify those actions.

Here are some ground-level descriptions of ways you can bring your implementation communications down to terra firma.

GETTING DOWN TO GROUND LEVEL

Imagine the following scenario. Bio Corp developed an innovative medical technology and created a whole new market that it has been able to dominate for a decade. Its leadership position enabled the firm to enjoy sizeable profit margins on its products. Now it's seeing new firms enter the market, using newer technologies and offering lower prices.

Fortunately for Bio, its competitors have quality problems. When it comes to healthcare, quality is a paramount concern, so most customers are still willing to pay Bio's higher prices. But Bio Corp's senior leaders recognize that in a year or two the quality gap will disappear, so the firm needs to develop a new strategic advantage to retain customers. Creating brand loyalty by building strong relationships with its customers seems to be the answer to maintaining market share. Therefore, the leaders launch a major initiative to focus on customers.

As described at the launch and in all the internal corporate communications, customer focus has been added as a key value of Bio's mission statement. In a major speech, the Bio CEO, Maggie, talked about the importance of having employees understand and believe in the importance of being customer focused. She recognized, she said, that this was a significant cultural shift because it would affect not only marketing and sales but also research and development. Scientists and engineers, for example, would need to involve their customers from the beginning of the product development cycle. They'd need to create products that served important customer needs rather than creating products they personally thought were cool.

Maggie asked employees to adopt a whole new mindset about how they saw their customers. Customers were to be viewed positively as partners rather than demanding children or an abstract "them." She concluded by promising that if all employees made a commitment to dramatically improve how they treat customers, they would change Bio Corp's culture and it would continue to be the world leader in its market niche.

It was a great talk and employees did feel Maggie's passion. But it was also a very high-level speech. She had talked about *new values and beliefs,* the need to have *a different mindset* and *a positive attitude,* and, especially, that employees need to be *committed*—those are all 30,000- and 40,000-foot terms. That's fine for the initial strategic communications, but now it was time to execute. To implement those lofty goals and make them an everyday reality, everyone needs to translate the high-level terms down to ground level.

One of the best ways to bring the big words down to reality is to ask a series of questions. To see how these questions work, imagine a Bio Corp middle manager named Dev who leads a group of product-development engineers and scientists. How could he make the new value a reality? Instead of thinking of ways to persuade employees of the importance of being customer focused, Dev decides he wants to get them activated. To do that he has to focus on ground-level actions to help the team get started.

What Do You Want People to Do?

This is the fundamental question. Sometimes when you ask that basic question you'll be able to spell out the exact actions you want people to begin doing and the ones you want them to stop doing. If this first question enables you to immediately state your goals at ground level, be happy. The question has done exactly what it was supposed to do. Your ground-level answers are perfect for activating behavior. There's no need to go back and come down through all of the other altitude levels. You've already taken the nonstop route to terra firma implementation and that's where you want to be.

Often when we're just learning to use the communication altimeter, this question usually produces answers that are still up in the clouds. Dev is no exception because he says, "I want them to walk the talk by really getting involved and partnering with our customers." Being "involved" and "partnering" are worthy objectives, but they don't tell the scientists and engineers exactly what they should be doing.

In What Situations?

Asking a second question can usually break the high-altitude holding pattern. In what situations should people be acting differently? The goal here is to develop a list of situations in which people could begin acting differently; it is not to describe how they should act.

Dev responds that he wants his team to act differently every time they're dealing with a customer. "Every time" is a general description of his goal, but it isn't a list of specific situations. Recognizing he needs to get closer to ground level, Dev modifies his question slightly and asks himself, what are some of the specific times or situations that team members actually come in contact with customers?

"When they're answering customer's inquiries."
"When they're talking to customers on the phone."
"When they're exchanging e-mails."
"When they're in product planning meetings with customers."

Posing the question in terms of listing specific situations, Dev is able to generate a list of settings in which his team members could begin living the new value of emphasizing the customer.

Remembering that the key to successful implementation is focus-focus-focus, Dev wisely picks only one from the list of situations in which to begin the change. He's trying to decide which situations are most important as well as the ones in which the change has the greatest likelihood of success. The product-planning meetings, he decides, are important and are where it should be possible to successfully make some small changes right away.

Having focused on customer planning meetings, Dev now tries to get even more specific by breaking the meetings with customers into subparts. Essentially, he's listing aspects of the meetings in which team members should act differently. His first answer is "anytime a customer is talking." Seeing that universal word *anytime*, he catches himself and asks, What are some of the specific times customers are talking during meetings?

"When customers are making suggestions about product modifications."

"When customers are complaining about aspects of our existing products."

"When customers are making suggestions about possible new products."

Dev realizes that "new product suggestions" are the most important of the three. With this more specific focus in mind, he returns to the first question: what should employees do when a customer makes a product suggestion? The moment he mentally poses the question he realizes he should subdivide the situation even further. He decides to distinguish between how they should react when a customer makes a suggestion the team perceives as (1) good, (2) questionable, or (3) unworkable.

Being a quick learner, Dev sees that each of these answers could be specified even further. Are there different kinds of good suggestions, questionable suggestions, and bad suggestions? He thinks, for example, that a product idea could be questionable because it was too difficult to manufacture, the market would be too small, it would be too costly to develop, and that it might never really be profitable.

Pleased with the way he is coming down to ground level, Dev realizes his first concern should be how employees react to good suggestions. He decides he'll get specific later about how the team should react to questionable and unworkable suggestions. Good ideas are hard to come by and he says to himself, "I want our people to really listen when customers propose a good idea."

As he repeats the answer to himself, he realizes that although he has been very specific about describing one part of conversations with customers, an important word is still up at least at 10,000 feet. Which one? *Listen*. What does he mean by listen?

He returns to the basic question and applies it to listening. What would people be doing if they were to listen carefully?

"Paying attention."

"Really thinking about what the customer is saying."

"Being open-minded."

What do you think of these answers? Is Dev getting lower or is he heading higher? After thinking of these definitions of listening, he sees that he is back up at the 30,000-foot psychological level by talking about being open-minded, thinking, and paying attention.

How Would You Know?

Spontaneously, Dev jumps to another question that can be helpful in getting down to earth. "How would I know if they were paying attention?" He then thinks about the question slightly differently. "What would it look like or what would I see them do, if they were paying attention?"

Conjuring an image of himself paying attention, Dev tries to analyze this picture. First, he'd be looking the customer in the eye. He wouldn't be looking out the window, at his notes, or at someone else. Second, he'd occasionally nod his head up and down as the customer was talking. He'd have a smile on his face, no looks of puzzlement or skepticism. Third, he'd be quiet and not say anything to interrupt the person. Dev thinks that might be too unnatural. He'd be giving voice to the occasional "ummhh" or "yeah," but no sentences. Imagining his staff, he pictures them saying "cool," because they still use that word to describe anything from a free bagel in the morning to receiving a big annual bonus.

"Now, if this is what they do while the customer is talking, what do they do when she stops talking?" he ponders. The quick answer that comes to mind is, "Well, they should respond." This makes him feel pretty good about himself, but then he realizes he is back up in the high-altitude zone.

Dev is stunned by how he so naturally fell into using "respond," an ambiguous 40,000-foot word even as he was trying to be grounded. He is so stunned that he starts talking out loud to himself. "Chuck would tell a customer the idea was 'unrealistic.' And when I later told him he shouldn't have said that, he'd say, 'Well, you told me to respond and that was my response. The idea is unrealistic, and I told him so.'"

Immediately, Dev knows he meant to say, "respond positively." And just as quickly he understands that simply saying he wants them to respond "positively" doesn't really help people get their feet on the ground. "Positive" is still nonspecific. He poses the same questions to himself again. "What would positive look like?" and "What would they be doing if they were responding positively?" Several answers spring to mind. Be enthusiastic. Act interested. Show that they like it.

Oops! Back up to high-altitude words, he thinks. Dev also knows he has to ask the question again. "What would I see them doing if they acted enthusiastic, interested, and showed they like the idea?" All he could think of were other generalities: be positive, get excited, and be enthused. Realizing he is going in circles, he tries a different approach.

What Would a Good Performer Do?

When you have trouble stating the behaviors in specific terms, this is another question you can ask to help you get down to ground level. Imagine someone on the team who epitomizes the high-level word you're trying to define. In this example Dev needs to think of someone who really does listen to people.

When you can picture someone responding "positively to a customer's good idea," you can usually also imagine the exact words they might say. Dev thought of Wendy, who really is a good listener. He could hear her saying, "Great idea" or, "I like that" or, "That's really insightful.

Good thinking." He realized there were many simple positive statements the team members could make.

Then Dev pictured himself. "I think of myself as being really caring about customers, but what does that mean? What would I say if I liked someone's idea?" Although his answers weren't that different from Wendy's, he realized that imagining exactly what he himself would say is another way to get down in the grass.

What's First, Second, Third?

Asking what team members should do after they expressed pleasure, Dev had inadvertently hit upon another great question for getting down to ground level. You can break the team's new behaviors down into a sequence by asking, "What is the first thing they should say or do? What could they do next? And what after that, and so on?"

After listening to the customer's suggestion, they might ask the person to elaborate. "How would you see that working?" Or going off in a different direction they could ask, "What do you see as the benefits of that kind of product?"

While there are many questions that could be asked, Dev thought of something else that should come second. After expressing pleasure with the customer's idea, his employees should next make sure they understand exactly what is being proposed. Immediately, Dev realized he has to be more specific about the behaviors involved in "making sure they understand."

Imagining how he would make sure he understood, he could hear himself telling the customer what he understood her to be saying. Then he thinks it would be good to conclude the summary by asking the customer, "Is that what you meant?"

Getting excited about his success in talking at ground level, Dev's mind races ahead to other things that should happen in a planning meeting with customers. In this context, the question became, "What should our team members do even before the meeting starts? And as soon as the meeting begins, what should they do next to show their focus on the customer?"

To the first question he answers: A day or two before the meeting, team members should call or e-mail each customer to reconfirm the meeting. They should also tell the customer that they're looking forward to working with them.

To the second question, he thinks, "At the very start of the meeting they should. . ."

"...have each customer and team member give his or her name and job function."

"...express gratitude that all these customer representatives were willing to come to the meeting."

"...acknowledge that the goal of the meeting is to encourage new ideas, not to squelch even what may seem like improbable suggestions."

"...spell out the agenda for the meeting, including time parameters."

The list kept growing and growing as Dev saw how useful it could be to ask questions about what comes first, second, third, etc. By thinking of the behavior change as a series of small steps, he could more easily describe each step in ground-level language.

Reflections

As Dev thought back over his use of the questioning technique, he became discouraged by how much he thinks and talks in high-level language. Clearly, this is going to be a behavior change for him. His 40,000-foot answers are examples of the kinds of mistakes anyone could make upon entering Stage 2 of the personal J Curve associated with learning to talk at ground level.

At the same time, he realized the many benefits of communicating in down-to-earth language. Obviously, it is going to be so much easier for employees to change the way they treat customers if he gives one or two ground-level suggestions instead of repeating his stratospheric speeches about the need to be more customer-focused.

Another important benefit comes from communicating in such a way that employees know exactly what to do. They'd be much more likely to try it, even if they thought it might be awkward or hard. Doing a specific action isn't going to be that hard and certainly isn't as frightening. The more they try, the quicker they'll do it successfully and the faster they'll make the new behaviors part of their standard operating procedure.

Dev remembered with amazement how words like *listen, pay attention,* and *be enthusiastic*, which he thought he understood, could be defined ever more specifically. He also sees how much more clearly he will be able to communicate with the team if he suggests that they "Look the customer in the eye when she's talking. Don't interrupt or say anything. Nod your head up and down."

As he thinks over the experience, Dev reminds himself that getting down to ground level just involves asking himself a set of simple questions:

What do you want the person to do?
What are some of the situations in which the person should start doing it?
What would a really good performer do in a particular situation?
How would you know that she had done it?
What would it look like?
What should the person do first, second, third, and so forth?

He can then apply his mental altimeter. When he gets an answer that isn't down to earth, he just needs to keep asking questions until he gets to ground level.

Dev figures that the scientists and engineers will have a much better idea of exactly how they are supposed to act if he talks at ground level than if he talks about being "customer-focused" or "really listening to the customer." In fact, most of his team would probably resent it if he told them to pay attention, because they think they already *are* paying attention.

Micromanaging

Telling employees exactly what they should and should not do is sometimes called micromanaging, a pejorative term. Talking at ground level is, in a sense, micromanaging, but that is sometimes necessary. Take, for instance, when talking with the Resisters.

At the beginning of a change, those who are resisting need clear, precise directions. They *are* going to need the leader's help; otherwise, they won't change. The best way the leader can help them get started along the path of change is by suggesting specific, ground-level behaviors they could use to be more customer-focused. So, for these employees, micromanaging has a place in the early stages of implementation. Once Resisters convert to adherents, the leader can return to a normal, less directive style of managing.

On the other hand, experienced team members and some of the Ready to Where people won't need such explicit suggestions. They probably already have their own ideas of specific ways to be more customer-focused. It may not be necessary to communicate at ground level with these employees, even at the beginning.

Dev smiles as he thinks of team members starting to actually treat customers differently. He pictures them coming back from a customer meeting telling him how useful the product-planning sessions were. Once a team experiences that kind of success, they'll be willing to try other changes. He can see that in fairly short order the team really will become more focused on the customers. And by now he knows how to define customer focus at every altitude level.

Although he made mistakes along the way in getting to ground level, Dev is learning how to identify the generalizations as soon as he says them, sometimes even as he thinks of them. He realizes that the real skill was catching them and redefining. He doesn't have to be perfect. When it comes to implementation, he reminds himself that "It's fine to start at the high altitude, but you just can't stay there."

Dev also realizes that he's only begun giving ground-level definitions of customer focus in one small situation. He'll have to go back and spell out customer-focused behaviors in other situations. This will be a continuing process. And at ground level, being customer-focused could mean an infinite number of things. Doing all this will take time and more work, but he only has to help the team do it at the beginning. Once they get over the emotional cliff and start up the other side, the team will be creating their own definitions.

Best of all, by Stage 4 they will also have changed how they feel and think about being customer-focused. By that point they will have adopted the idea of "focusing on the customer" as simply "the way we do business at Bio Corp," and it will have become one of the company's core values.

Chapter

6

ASK, DON'T TELL

As head of the new cost-reduction effort, Jeneen is excited about the plan the special task force has created and the savings that will result. It's all the more satisfying to her because two prior teams created good plans but could never get them implemented. She's confident it's going to be different this time.

The difference is that Jeneen made sure the plan detailed exactly how the manager and employees in each department should implement the plan. Every step has been spelled out in ground-level language. All they have to do is follow the plan exactly as it has been given to them to produce dramatic results.

What's your guess? Do you think Jeneen's ground-level plan is going to work? I'm worried that this plan will also fail. Why? Because the people who will have to implement the change haven't been involved in deciding upon the details of the plan. Telling people exactly how to do what they're supposed to do can produce disastrous consequences.

Resistance often results when we spell out each step someone is to take. That's because most of us think of ourselves as skilled professionals who deserve some control over how we do our jobs. We take pride in knowing how to do our work. We want to be respected for our abilities and it's almost insulting to be told exactly how to proceed.

Here's the manager's practical dilemma: people are more likely to initiate a change if the steps are specified at ground level, but when people are told exactly what to do they resent it and rebel. Fortunately, there's a simple solution to the conundrum. Ask them what to do. Instead of telling, ask a question such as:

"How would you approach this?"
"What are your ideas about how we should do this?"
"Can you see any ways we could make this work?"

Asking rather than telling has many advantages. Most obvious are the motivational benefits. An employee who has a voice in defining how to solve a problem has a much stronger desire to make the solution work.

Probably even more important, employees, when asked, often come up with new and better ideas. Many of their ideas may not be feasible, but you only need one or two that are. The time costs of explaining why their weak ideas won't work will be more than outweighed by the benefits of adopting the good ones.

This chapter will detail ways to make the question-and-answer process more genuine and thus create involvement, which is an important element of activation. While many managers give lip service to "empowering" or "involving" workers in designing change, often they don't understand that the way to do that is by posing questions rather than issuing orders. It's especially important to keep asking in Stages 2 and 3 when unexpected hurdles appear and mistakes are common.

Too often, leaders, when they query the rank and file for their ideas, have already chosen a path and really are seeking ratification, not alternatives. None of us like to be treated as a rubber stamp.

If you're going to ask, you must also listen. Otherwise, employees will interpret your questions as a gimmick meant to trick them into thinking that your plan is actually their idea. You must be sincerely interested in their answers. And there is good reason to be sincerely interested. Why wouldn't you be interested in listening to someone who has an idea that could save you time and money on implementation? Using people's suggestions and giving them credit for their contributions are the most sincere forms of listening.

Involving employees this way helps reduce the negative emotions that block change. Being involved in deciding what steps to take gives workers more courage and confidence. Plus, it motivates people to prove that their idea will work.

As a leader you're accustomed to being the one who selects goals and decides how to achieve them. Using the "Ask, Don't Tell" approach could require a major change in your management style. While the frontline people want a voice in how to implement a strategy, you may be resistant to encouraging them to speak out. Here is another change you may have to make and another personal J Curve you'll have to go through. Let's break the "Ask, Don't Tell" approach down to ground level so that it's easy for you to get started.

THE *JEOPARDY* TECHNIQUE

The television show *Jeopardy* differs from all other quiz shows. On other programs the contestants try to answer the quiz master's questions. On *Jeopardy*, the host gives the answer and the contestants must come up with the question. It's done with the word magic of placing the phrases such as "*Who was...*" or "*What is...*" in front of the answer.

This game show device can serve as a good reminder of a helpful technique for implementing change. Anytime you're tempted to give an answer, ask a question instead, especially when you know the answer. When you think you know the best (only) way things should be done, a warning light should go off. Almost always, multiple paths exist to any goal. So before committing to your plan, find out if anyone has a different and better idea. Ultimately, your idea may turn out to be superior, but it's worth the time to see if anyone has a suggestion that is even better.

Another time you should ask rather than tell is when you are deciding what's best for someone else, especially a group of people. We're often tempted to make autocratic decisions when we regard ourselves as experts in the field. Let's say, for example, you know a great deal about training and development. So you, and possibly an outside consultant, may decide what kind of training a particular work group requires. Without involving the group, the two of you design the educational program, appoint the instructors, and decide upon scheduling.

This tendency is easy to overcome if you use the Golden Rule and think about how you would like to be treated. We'd all like to be consulted before someone else decides our fate. Do unto others by including them in helping specify exactly how to go about achieving the goal.

Another time to be sure to ask rather than tell is after a mistake has been made. Mistakes trigger a strong tendency to tell people what they should have done and how they should act in the future. Aside from temporarily making you feel better, what good does this do? Whether embarrassed about their mistake, or angry at your reprimand, everyone's attention is so consumed with feelings that they don't hear your advice.

Challenging as it may be, resist the temptation to tell. Instead, give the person a few moments to recover from the error and then ask, "What ideas do you have about how to handle that kind of thing in the future?" or "What practical lessons did you gain from that experience?" Instead of a paternalistic lecture that degrades the person's ability, these questions show a continuing confidence in the individual. Asking rather than lecturing will earn you the employee's gratitude even if it doesn't produce new solutions.

Obviously, you want to ask rather than tell *before* implementing a change, but it's also important to keep asking *during* implementation. That's especially true during Stages 2 and 3 when unexpected barriers are encountered. Those doing the actual implementing know the most about the situation and probably will have the best ideas about how to deal with it. You can make the inevitable midcourse corrections more efficiently if you use those who are directly involved as your expert "consultants."

Sure, some situations are emergencies and require quick action. So it's natural to resort to telling in those instances. But the next day it may be useful to review what happened and ask people for their recommendations on how to handle a comparable situation if it were to occur again.

Putting the *Jeopardy* Method into Practice

Imagine that the executive team has decided that the single most important goal for the new year is to boost sales. Every business unit has been given the task of coming up with new product lines or new markets for existing lines. This is a radical change for an organization accustomed to taking orders and not having to fight for every sales dollar.

Mary, one of your direct reports, has only been a member of your group for six months. She's highly motivated and has already made significant contributions. During a private meeting with you, she proposes the idea of using retail outlets for a product line that in the past has only been sold to original equipment manufacturers. It's an intriguing idea but one that you know is fraught with challenges.

Mary is new to the firm and to the industry, and she's never done anything like this before. You're very impressed with her abilities and you decide to give her the go-ahead, but what are you going to say to her?

Many bosses would assume the mantle of wise senior advisor and lay out how Mary should tackle this assignment. In other words, they'd tell her what to do. It's easy to fall into that default mode of telling. After all, you're more experienced, and you are only trying to help her. And, quite honestly, it's nice to demonstrate your knowledge to a younger person.

Despite your good intentions and the possible benefits of telling Mary how to proceed, what else could you do? Yes, begin by *asking* Mary what steps she would take to start moving her idea forward. You can always give her your ideas after encouraging her with a chance to tell you hers.

Mary suggests that the first step is to do preliminary research on the idea's feasibility. When that's done, she thinks the second step would be to form an interdepartmental team to evaluate the data and decide on a plan. You're impressed with her answers because her thoughts are running parallel to yours, although you hadn't thought of involving employees from other departments in these early stages. Already, asking has begun to pay off.

As Mary thinks about these first two steps, she's a little overwhelmed because it's going to be a lot of work and she still has her regular job duties to perform. You might help her use her ingenuity to break this project down into doable segments that fit her schedule. You can ask her questions about each of the two steps she's proposed.

The following are some general guidelines for asking questions that can be applied in a wide range of situations.

Go for the Verbs

Our description of the steps in implementation plans is almost always stated in general terms. To help people get started, it's important to bring the plan down to ground-level language. Take Mary's two ideas: "do feasibility research" and "assemble a team to decide on a plan for moving forward."

The verb that needs to be broken down in the first step is "do"; in the second step, the verbs are both "assemble" and "decide." The format for your questions could be What would be involved in *verb*? or How would you go about *verb*? Using these verbs as examples, here are some questions you might pose to Mary. "What would be involved in doing the research?" or "How would you go about assembling a team and how would the team arrive at a decision?"

Whether you are dealing with employees who are already on board or those who are resisting a change, it's good practice to get the *verbs* in any plan down to ground level. You probably already have one idea about how something should be done. By asking for other people's ideas, you'll be able to consider alternative approaches.

Dissect the Nouns

In the same way you asked Mary to break down the verbs, you can also invite her to break down the nouns or noun phrases: *feasibility research, team,* and *a plan for moving forward* "What would be included in the *feasibility research*?" "What are you looking for in the *team*?" "What would be the important elements of the *plan for moving forward*?"

Anticipate Problems

Unexpected problems arise in any endeavor. As Mary is answering your questions, you may think of your own experiences. Ask yourself what problems you've encountered in comparable situations in the past. For example, as Mary talks about the Web sites she'll use in conducting the research, you might think of a time when you overlooked some internal documents when doing background research on a project.

Although it's tempting to tell her what she should examine, try asking for her ideas. "Can you think of any existing documents in our own files that might be worth reviewing before you begin the Internet research?" In addition to the ones you thought of, she may suggest others. If she doesn't, probe again and encourage her to think about any of the organization's recent projects that might be relevant. If she still draws a blank, you can then explicitly recommend some specific ones for her to consider.

Or you could begin with a general question such as "What problems might arise as you're...doing the research, assembling the team, creating the plan?" When she identifies potential problems, you can then ask her, rather than tell her, how she would deal with them.

A slightly different approach is to begin by suggesting a potential problem and then asking the other person how she would handle it. For example, as Mary is describing how she's going to assemble a team, you might comment that the talented employees she wants to include on the team could feel they're too overcommitted to serve on yet another project. Here as well, you can ask instead of tell. "Can you think of any key people you want on the team who might feel they are already doing too many special projects? What could you do to make being on your team less onerous and more interesting to them?" Give the person time to think of an answer before saying anything more. It may take a minute, but she'll probably generate some clever solutions. If not, then you can give her yours.

Inquire about Desired Outcomes

Inquiring about the desired results can also be helpful. You might ask Mary, "How will you summarize your research findings?" Or "What will the team's action plan look like?" If needed, you can delve more deeply. "Are there certain aspects of the research results that you want to highlight, and how could you do that?" or "What things definitely need to be addressed in the plan?"

Because the results of any endeavor often need to be shared, it can be useful to ask about subsequent communications. "Are there any people who will need to receive the research results, and what would be the best way to get that information to them?"

Specify the Parameters

Following the old journalistic guidelines for news writing, you can ask *who, what, where,* and *when* types of questions to elicit more details. This is especially useful in taking an action step that has been described in terms ranging from 20,000 or 10,000 feet down to ground level.

- "Who will do the research?"
- "What kind of information will they be looking for?"
- "Where will they look for information?"
- "When will they do the research?"
- "Who will assemble the team?"
- "What are the critical parts of the process of assembling a team?"
- "How long will it take to assemble the team?"

Sometimes you can ask an even more focused question that will get the 500-foot answers down into the grass. For example, "Okay, given that the research will take about eight hours, will you do it all in one day or would you prefer a few hours over several days?" Resist the temptation to tell Mary to do it all at once, or to segment it, and instead let her come up with an approach that works for her.

STYLES OF ASKING

Once you get accustomed to asking rather than telling, you can refine your style by following the guidelines described in this section.

Interrogation

When you begin using the *Jeopardy* technique of asking rather than telling, it's easy to sound like an attorney conducting a cross-examination. What does *assemble* mean? Exactly how would you do the research? Springing such a list of questions on an employee can be overwhelming.

It's not just the questions that can be intimidating. Your nonverbal behavior, especially a sour facial expression, can frighten people. Smiling instead of frowning, keeping your eyes wide open rather than narrowing them are just a couple of the small things you can do to subtly encourage people to relax when answering your questions.

Your manner is critical to establishing an environment that puts the other person at ease. You want to have a dialogue, even if your role is largely to ask questions and to listen to the other person's answers. The key is to ask questions in a way that shows you respect the employee's abilities rather than implying that you think you know all the answers.

Treat other people as your peers as you try to help them break down the change into manageable substeps. Be open to their ideas and be willing to learn new ways of doing things. When they respond to your questions, be accepting, not judgmental, and affirm their answers.

Remember that your goal is to help them generate new and better answers than those you already have in mind. Express your praise and gratitude when they come up with new ways to implement the project.

During this dialogue you'll probably also be stimulated to think of novel ideas yourself. It's fine to tell people your new ideas but wait until they've had a chance to voice theirs. When you do share your creative insights, make sure to remind them that it was the conversation with them that spurred your creativity. This is another way of acknowledging their contribution.

In a sense you are coaching them through the process. Don't think of yourself as the kind of coach who knows all the answers. Instead, see yourself as a facilitator who is good at asking questions that bring forth the knowledge of others and who is sincerely interested in hearing their answers.

Leading Questions

Your style also is reflected in the kinds of questions you ask. It is so tempting to indirectly tell by reframing your answer as a question:

"Don't you think you should...?"
"Does it make sense to...?"
"Would it be useful to...?"

Leading questions show a lack of respect for the other person. People will quickly see through your tactic even if you aren't consciously aware of what you're doing. When they realize your questions are really telling them the answer you want them to give, they'll withdraw. They'll avoid answering your questions because they feel you are being patronizing—and you *are*. Don't do it. Learn to sincerely help them generate their ideas

Condemning Questions

Avoid questions that implicitly convey your negative judgment on the person's previous answer. Imagine that Gary gives you his ideas about what should be on the agenda for a team meeting. You think his suggestion would be a serious mistake, and you're about to tell him so. Remembering to ask rather than tell, you force yourself to phrase it as a question such as:

"Would you really think of doing something like that?"
"Why would you do that?"
"Don't you see the problems that would cause?"

The condemnation is virtually dripping off your inquiries. These questions are simply vehicles to carry your disapproval. You're criticizing his solution rather than trying to encourage more ideas. In popular language you "shot down" Gary's answer, and the effect will be to silence him as well as other members of the team.

This is not to say that all suggestions are good ones. Everyone occasionally comes up with bad ideas, and those must be analyzed and rejected. But immediately analyzing an answer you think is problematic will stop the process of generating more ideas. Mentally note their answers and keep probing for more suggestions. After they run out of recommendations, you can return to the ones you didn't think were useful.

You'll want to explicitly discuss the potential problems with their suggestion, but you can still use questions. Explain your concerns and then ask for ideas about how to avoid the problems that you've described.

For example, Mario proposes offering first-time customers a greatly reduced price on one product line to increase business. Your concern is that existing customers could feel as though they are being mistreated. You might say to Mario, "I can see how your idea would be attractive to new customers, but it makes me worry that our existing customers might feel they are being overcharged when they have to pay full price. Can you think of any ways to do what you're proposing without alienating our existing customers?"

If you're worried about several negative consequences of an employee's proposal, tell him each one in sequence and ask for his solution. "Your idea has many advantages, but I'm concerned about several possible disadvantages. Maybe you can help me work through each one. For starters, this could dramatically affect profitability this quarter. How would we deal with that?"

Often employees give impractical answers because you didn't fully explain all of the constraints in the situation. In these instances you can say something such as "Your idea is a good one, but it makes me realize that I forgot to tell you an important boundary condition. We have to do this without any added costs. I apologize for not explaining that critical detail. Given this restriction, how else could we approach this?"

In general, it's better to postpone these discussions about the pros and cons of a particular suggestion until the person or group has had time to think of as many ideas as possible. If you stop to assess each solution as it's proposed, you'll stifle the generation of suggestions. Put your concerns in your mental parking lot, and come back to them after the brainstorming is complete.

COMMON PROBLEMS AND SOLUTIONS

Asking rather than telling will yield great dividends; however, if you have a history of "telling," it may take people time to get accustomed to your new approach. Problems often pop up at the beginning of your transition from telling to asking.

Here's how to respond if your employees say nothing, give general answers, or say "just tell me."

Say Nothing

Their blank faces coupled with a shrugging of the shoulders imply they're devoid of any notion of what to suggest. In your experience, do these empty expressions accurately convey what is going on in their heads? Or do you suspect that despite their puzzled expressions, they do have ideas but aren't going to say a word?

We all know people who have things to say but don't want to say them. Why don't they? Maybe they're keeping quiet because of the way you reacted to suggestions in the past. They probably remember that your reaction to someone else's suggestions was quite stern and condemning. Fearing similar possible criticism, many people say nothing.

Actually, they probably remember something else about you. If they keep quiet long enough, what will you do? You'll give them the answer. You'll tell them your ideas about how to proceed. So they'll let you develop the plans, and they'll just sit back, nod, and tell you how clever you are after they've gotten you to do all the work. They've learned it's better to let you do it your way.

Sometimes employees will try to bait you into answering by asking, "Gee, I don't know. Where do you think we should start?" It may feel good to be asked and you may be tempted to answer, but redirect the question back to them. "I don't have any really good ideas on this one yet; that's why I'd like to hear yours."

One effective way to overcome this kind of silence is to just repeat the question. "So if we're going to hire a new project manager, how would we start?" If all you get are shrugs and looks of noncomprehension, simply repeat the question. "We're all agreed that we need to hire a manager to coordinate this project. How would we begin that hiring process?" It's nice if you can put the restatement in more engaging language, but it's not necessary. The second question can be worded almost the same as the first.

The exact words aren't crucial because the real message is conveyed not by the words you use but by the fact that you repeated the question. Your repetition communicates an underlying meaning: I *really* want to know your ideas.

Sometimes people will remain silent after several restatements of the general question. In these instances you can usually break the silence by being prepared to ask some specific questions:

"How should we describe the job in the advertisement?"
"Where should we place the ad?"
"How could we interest internal candidates as well as external ones?"

These more detailed questions make it hard for employees to act as if they don't have any ideas. When they do make suggestions, remember to be affirming of all answers so that your response encourages others to join in.

Give General Answers

"Okay, I'll tell you where the hiring starts; it begins with commitment. There have been too many times where we said we were going to do something, but then we never followed through. So, making a commitment is the first thing we have to do."

Hallelujah! At least you don't have to deal with a wall of silence. You got someone to talk and that's progress. Although you recognize that this answer is up at an altitude of 40,000 feet, don't say so. Anytime you get an answer, no matter how general, express some pleasure or agreement. "You're absolutely right; commitment is critical. And I can remember some of those great ideas that died because we didn't follow through. And I know who was responsible—me. So, yes, we must be committed. I'm assuming we are committed to making this happen, and I'd like your ideas on what we should do to make our commitment a reality."

Or agree with the other person's general answer and then follow up with a question about specific steps to take. For example, "Agreed, we need to be committed to quickly making a good hire. What kind of educational background and experience would the person have?" These follow-up questions can be directed at the employee who gave the initial general answer or to the whole group. When you're working with a group of people, you want to stimulate everyone to begin making ground-level suggestions.

Say "Just Tell Me"

"Look boss, we know you. You have this thing all planned out, so why don't you save us a lot of time and tell us *your* plan?" Often when people say this, it's embarrassing because it's the truth. You do have a plan, and you probably believe it's a great one.

Although you have your own ideas, you shouldn't tell them yours first. Once they hear your ideas, many of these employees will stop thinking and immediately agree. Others will be subtly influenced by what you say so they won't be able to generate any novel approaches.

In these instances in which you already have ideas, you can encourage others to talk first by saying something such as, "You're right. I do have some ideas but they're only my ideas. I'd like to hear what you think. Often when we learn what somebody else has thought, it biases the way we think about it from that point on. I'd like you to approach this fresh and unbiased. After you've had a chance to express your ideas, I'll be glad to tell you mine. At that point we can evaluate all of them and see which ones make the most sense."

The "just tell us your ideas" response can also be awkward when you don't have the slightest idea of what to do. This is another perfect time for honesty. Openly admit you don't have a solution and let them know how important their role is by proposing ideas.

SHOWING SINCERITY

Asking rather than telling will be perceived as a manipulative gimmick unless you are sincerely interested in everyone's answers. What could you do to show that you are sincere? If you remember why you're asking questions, it's easy to be sincere. You're asking because you hope they have a better answer. Therefore, you really want to listen to everything they say because they could give you a priceless solution at any moment.

Seasoned managers learn how to use questions to elicit the answers they want to hear. When workers give an unwelcome suggestion, the manager might say something such as "Yes, well, that's one possibility. Who has another idea?" But when the manager gets a desired answer, he says, "Great suggestion"—and doesn't bother asking for more ideas. Your employees learn to pick up on your cues, and they'll figure out the suggestions you like and which ones you don't. You may as well be *telling* because that's the effect of your verbal and nonverbal responses to their answers. Actually it's worse than telling, because people resent you for acting as though they're not smart enough to see through your tactic.

Asking isn't an adequate demonstration of sincerity; you must use their suggestions. Fortunately, employees usually have good ideas and you'll gladly want to include them. Even in cases where you aren't certain of the value of what they're saying, if it is not that costly to you, it's probably a good idea to include some of their suggestions. Who knows? You may be wrong in your appraisal, and what they've proposed may turn out to be very workable.

In addition to including their ideas, it's important to explicitly communicate the fact that you've changed the plan to incorporate their suggestion. You can do this when the idea is put forward by saying, "That's a sensational idea. I didn't think of that. Yes, we'll definitely want to do that instead of what I had planned. Thanks."

It's also important to identify people's suggestions later when you are celebrating the success of the plan. In addition to recognizing their contribution, you're telling everyone else that in the future you want them to participate in shaping the implementation. They'll get the implicit message that you're not only open to other people's ideas but that you actually use those ideas and happily give credit to the originators. Acknowledging those contributions is one of the best ways to build teamwork, and it will make people want to be on your team.

PRACTICAL ADVICE

The repeated point of this chapter is Ask, Don't Tell. That good advice will remain only an idea for you unless you put it into action. The way to do that is to follow the route of activation.

You can bring this idea down to ground-level steps by deciding upon three concrete situations in which you will apply it. Select individuals or groups with whom you have a history of telling rather than asking. The individuals might be people at your workplace or in your personal life. The group might be a team of which you are a leader or a member.

For each instance, imagine an upcoming situation in which your first impulse would be to tell them what they should do. In order to prepare yourself to act differently, be specific about the time and place in which the situation is likely to arise. Perhaps you have an appointment scheduled with an employee, a meeting planned with the team, or an opportunity to speak with your child at dinner tomorrow. Picture what things you will be tempted to tell them, and between now and then, rehearse some questions you could ask instead.

Is there someone you have to contact to ascertain progress on a project? As you call him, you're already anticipating a problem he's going to encounter and you already know how he should deal with the problem. Resist the temptation to tell him your solution. As he tells you about the problem, think of questions you could ask to get him thinking about solutions. "What ideas do you have about dealing with this?" or "Have you thought of any ways to resolve this issue?" By asking questions you're teaching problem-solving, developing the employee's independence, and delegating work. It's a win-win approach.

Group meetings provide an ideal environment in which to practice asking. Typically, an issue is raised and several people, including you, have opinions about what should be done. Too often we just impatiently wait for the others to finish their remarks. We think, "Why don't they quit talking so I can give the right answer?" Instead, while you're waiting, think of questions you could ask to pull more answers from the other group members. After others have made their suggestions, you can insert your idea if no one else has thought of it. By asking, you adopt the role of a team member who really is promoting teamwork rather than attempting to gain personal glory. This is an approach you can use whether you're the group leader or a member.

At first people may be surprised by your questions, simply because they're accustomed to your being more direct. You may have to repeat your questions to show that you're sincerely interested in what they think. Once you demonstrate that you would really like to hear their ideas, you'll get more of them. And, most likely, you'll be surprised by how insightful and clever their ideas are.

Just as it will take others a little time to adjust to your new behavior, it may take you several tries to change your style. In yet another illustration of the J Curve, you may not be very consistent when you first begin. You may slip and resort to telling. That's normal in Stage 2. Also, your initial questions may meet with blank stares or discussions that aren't very fruitful. The key is to keep doing it.

If you will continue to question, you'll soon gain skill and start to reap big rewards. You'll get new and better ideas, you'll feel better about your coworkers, and they'll be much happier to be working with you. You'll realize how clever and thoughtful people can be and how much there is to gain from encouraging them to talk.

Chapter

7

FRONT-LOAD THE REWARDS

Think for a moment about the five stages of the J Curve. When does it become really worthwhile to have made a change? When does the really big payoff occur? Not until Stage 5. That's when your performance surpasses what it was back when you began in Stage 1. At the end, it becomes profitable to have gone through all the costs of making the change.

The nature of life is that we get the rewards of change at the end. Our nature as human beings is to want and need rewards at the beginning. This is a disconcerting discontinuity. We want and need the rewards in Stages 2 and 3 when performance is dropping and we're making one error after another. But because we are repeatedly failing, nature doesn't provide us with many morale boosters.

Listen to those words: *want* and *need*. To anyone with a salesperson's sensitivity, wants and needs translate into opportunities. And there is a golden opportunity for you, the leader of change, to provide the rewards when employees need them—at the beginning when things are going poorly. Consider this example.

While others are holding back, Christina in the Billing Department is trying her best to make the new procedure work. She's not convinced a new system is necessary or that, if one is required, this is the best method. She's embarrassed and frustrated because she was so good at doing things the old way. In her heart of hearts, she may at times wish she hadn't agreed to go along with the change. Still, she persists.

Christina, like everyone else, needs encouragement at the beginning when progress is slow, not just at the end when rewards are traditionally doled out. What could her manager do? Give her early and frequent customized praise.

Just as a parent cheers an infant taking his first steps even though a fall is sure to follow, the wise leader strongly supports people going through the tumult of Stages 1, 2, and 3. Yes, like the baby, they're going to stumble. But when they gain their balance, whole new possibilities will open up.

This chapter explains how a leader—without showing favoritism, appearing unprofessional, or insincere—can "turbocharge" the impact of praise by tailoring it to each individual. By sincerely expressing approval of even the smallest steps in the new direction, leaders can help motivate people to persist with the new approach through the most difficult and discouraging phases of change.

The term "front-loading rewards" sounds cold and objective. While the phrase accurately captures the idea, it certainly doesn't express the human feelings behind this managerial imperative. Take the example of Christina in Billing. What's it like to be in her shoes as she takes those small, cautious steps down the side of the emotional cliff in Stage 2? Though she has doubts about your proposed change, she's still willing to act even if she finds it painful to commit errors. Her willingness is all the more admirable because her performance would have been error-free if she were doing it the old way. At times Christina probably thinks about the benefits she's giving up, and she senses the opportunity cost of rewards forgone.

And why is she going through all of this? Because of you. When you look at the situation from her perspective, you see that what she's doing is very special and deserves your gratitude. Identifying what your employees are going through in Stages 1 and 2 as they face their change "monsters" should help spark your gratitude. It should also remind you to redouble your efforts to express your admiration and praise for even their smallest efforts. As managers we'd do well to emulate the pride parents have in the accomplishments of their infant sons and daughters. Like those parents, we should shower our "family members" with recognition for their courage in being willing to try something new.

By front-loading praise and other rewards at the beginning of a change when nature isn't providing many incentives, we can help employees through the frustration of learning to do something new. Your praise enables people to acquire the skill and knowledge so they can be successful at the new way of doing things. When they begin to achieve success, they then experience the inherent benefits of doing things the new way. A personal transformation begins to happen in Stage 4 of the change process when employees will actually begin saying:

"This is fun."
"This does make the job easier."
"I actually prefer this way to the old one."

As the individual going through the change begins to experience the benefits of the new approach, you, the person facilitating the change, can gradually stop providing external rewards. During the later stages of change, people begin to develop their own intrinsic rewards for doing things the new way.

PERSONALIZING PRAISE

If you see the logic behind using praise in the beginning stages of a change, then how do you make sure that praise is as valuable as possible? There are some simple things you can do to dramatically increase the impact of your praise.

To be effective, praise has to be perceived as sincere. It requires that you have to mean it and that you have to communicate that you mean it. Sometimes even when you are sincere, it doesn't come out in the words you say. There's a straightforward way to communicate sincerity and to simultaneously turbocharge the effects of your praise. Personalize your praise by adding a sentence or two that expresses the exact nature of your pleasure. When you do, people will feel how much you care.

Notice the difference between these two expressions of praise for the same action.

> "Thanks, Jorge, great job."
>
> "Thanks, Jorge, great job. Because you did such high-quality work, it was possible for me to finish the proposal by the deadline."

There's nothing wrong with the first one, but the second will have much more impact because Jorge knows why his actions were important to you. By adding that brief explanatory sentence, you've made your praise much more meaningful. Which one is he more likely to repeat that evening over dinner with his family? He'll probably swell with pride as he recounts how critical his efforts were in making it possible for the boss to get an important job completed on time.

In a sense, general words of praise are at an altitude of 40,000 feet. They're going to have more impact if you can translate them down to ground level. Personalizing your praise means being specific about what the person did and exactly why it was praiseworthy.

A side benefit of personalizing your praise is that you create an easy opening to enhance the relationship. What might happen if you personalize the praise with a leading remark, such as "Thanks, Jorge, great work. You must have had to put in some extra hours."?

Jorge then will have the perfect opportunity to tell you how he had to come in several hours early each day and about the problems he encountered. Those details will give you a better appreciation of what he accomplished and a chance to sincerely express your gratitude in even greater detail. Most likely he'll end up thanking you for recognizing his efforts. This added discussion only takes a few more minutes; however, it strengthens the relationship because you better understand one another. Even if Jorge says, "Oh, it was nothing," you know he loves getting your added recognition.

Praise gives meaning to what someone did in the past but also makes it more likely he or she will do it again in the future. Praise reinforces an act, letting employees know you'd like them to repeat it. Personalizing your praise magnifies the power of your words. Workers will be motivated to do even more than they did in the past in order to garner more of your personal attention.

WHY DON'T WE PRAISE MORE?

Given its obvious importance and the fact that it takes so little time and money, why are people so stingy with their praise? Many managers resist the idea of openly expressing gratitude. They may claim it's not their nature to praise or that they're "not a people person." Let's examine some of these rationalizations.

Avoid Appearing Soft or Unprofessional

Under a definition of leadership spawned generations ago by the military and early industrial leaders, managers weren't supposed to show their feelings. Praise was interpreted as weakness and made all parties uncomfortable. Times have changed and so have leadership styles. The command-and-control approach that was all too common with manual laborers doesn't work in service industries or with highly skilled professionals. To be an inspiring leader, it's necessary to let people know how much regularly and honestly you value what they're doing.

Using personalized praise shows people what you care about most deeply, especially during a major change. It energizes and reaffirms the direction in which they should be headed. Your passion arouses their passion for the work ahead. Far from being soft, you'll be viewed as having real strength.

Avoid Showing Favoritism

It's true that once you start praising one or two people, others will want a pat on the back as well. What's wrong with that? As long as they are doing good work, it won't take that much time to tell them about it. After all, don't you take the time to tell them when their performance is subpar? Such criticism could easily lead to claims that a manager is biased, and yet managers continue to criticize. If anything, personalizing praise forces us to be more conscious of everyone's contribution and that should promote greater fairness.

This whole line of reasoning can be a distraction, however, because employees pay attention to far more than our verbal kudos or criticisms in judging whether a boss is fair. Promotions, assignments, and resource allocation play a far larger role.

Avoid the Impression of Being Overly Friendly or Ingratiatory

This sometimes arises in the context of male-female relationships or when a subordinate praises a superior. Misperceptions are usually engendered by words of praise that go beyond the bounds of the actual reality or become too personal. Repeated praising, especially with inflated language, raises red flags. Keeping personalized praise work-centered helps defend against this misperception. By specifying exactly what the person did to win your praise, you focus more on their actions than on them as people.

Praise Will Lose Its Value

This may be true when applied to the overuse of insincere praise, but that's not what's being recommended. Actually, by personalizing your praise, you increase its value. Your more detailed comments show you really *are* paying attention. Taking the added time to express such feelings magnifies its importance.

People Already Know

Maybe they do, but they never get tired of hearing it. Truth is, we're all gluttons for praise even though we may be occasionally uncomfortable or embarrassed while hearing it. Such public discomfort shouldn't stop you from offering personalized praise. You can give it in private or put it in a letter, but do it. Even top performers, who seem to be brimming with self-confidence, have times of personal doubt. At those moments, a pat on the back is especially meaningful.

They're Getting Paid and, Besides, They're Only Doing Their Job

The function of a monthly paycheck is not to provide regular feedback. You give constructive guidance by telling employees quite explicitly what they're doing right and wrong.

In the context of change, they're probably doing much more than what is required by their regular job description. They're taking on added duties, responsibility, and risk. Most likely you didn't increase the amount in their paycheck to account for those added duties. Regularly giving personalized praise, then, may be a convenient way to balance the books for all they're doing.

They'll Expect a Financial Reward

This concern often underlies the others. The fear is that words of praise will be met with "Well, put it in the paycheck" or "Then why isn't my salary higher?" Virtually no reasonable person says such things unless other serious problems exist in the relationship. In the unlikely case your praise does evoke such a reaction, take that as a signal to further explore their underlying concerns.

You might want to take their monetary request seriously. Perhaps what they did was of such importance that you should use money to show your gratitude. If not cash, maybe there's some other tangible way you could compensate them, such as time off or paying for a professional development program. In most instances though, the small actions you are praising are worthy of commendation but not compensation.

There are many ways to communicate such a message politely. "Yes, it might be nice to get a financial bonus for what you did. While your actions were significant and important, it's usually only when we achieve our major goals that we earn monetary compensation. My hope—and it's only a hope, not a guarantee—is that when we reach our big goal, there will be larger recognition of what we've all done. It may not be money, but we'll have to find some way to celebrate all the work that everyone has done to make this a success."

I DON'T KNOW HOW TO PRAISE

This next section is designed for managers who claim that it's a lack of knowledge, and not a lack of motivation, that stops them from praising people. You'll learn a variety of ways you can give your praise more personal impact. Making these changes in your communication style will benefit you as well as the people you work with.

How to Personalize Praise

Often a simple word of praise is enough.

> "Great work."
> "Good job."
> "Terrific idea."
> "Good for you."
> "Very impressive."
> "Thanks for handling that so well."

These brief, nonspecific expressions can be said with a variety of tones of voice, emphases, and nonverbal behaviors to underscore your feelings. To turbocharge the impact of your praise, you can expand and personalize it for particular individuals. To help you think of ways to bring your praise down to ground level, ask yourself any of the following questions before you actually speak. One of these is sure to stimulate you to think of a way to elaborate your praise.

- How have the person's actions helped you or the team?
- Why is their contribution especially helpful at this time?
- Exactly how did he or she do it?
- Are there many other people who would do something like this?
- What kind of effort did it take?
- What do their actions say about him or her as a person?
- What does their performance imply for the organization's future...and for his or her future?
- What does it say about their organization?

To see how to use these questions, we'll rely on two recurring examples. Imagine Leonor and Isaac, who have each done something praiseworthy in dealing with a change. Leonor has volunteered herself and her branch to be the guinea pigs in testing a new procedure. Isaac has brought more work on himself by volunteering to teach his new boss, Gene, the ins and outs of the operation because he was hired from the outside. The sample wordings are meant only as general illustrations and, naturally, you'll want to use phrases that suit your style and situation.

How Did Their Actions Help?

"Thank you so much for volunteering. Because you and your team are willing to take on that added work, Leonor, we can smooth out the kinks in the new procedure before we roll it out across the organization. That will save me the embarrassment of having to deal with all kinds of complaints."

"Way to go, Isaac. Since you're doing such a thorough job bringing Gene up to speed, I have time to work on the Ajax bid. That means a lot to me."

There are so many ways that another person's actions could have helped you. Their action might have saved you, or the organization, money or time. Their action might have done something to help you out of a tight situation or made you look good in other people's eyes.

Why Was Their Contribution So Important at That Time?

"I was starting to lose hope that we'd be able to give the new procedure a test run. When you volunteered your branch office, you really raised my spirits and renewed my hope."

"Isaac, the thought that I'd have to take all that time to train Gene had me feeling overwhelmed. Knowing that you are doing it so well has lifted a great weight off my back."

Another person's action can be especially important when that action may have helped avert an impending problem or crisis. The format here is to briefly describe the nature of the problem, how his or her action solved it, and how you felt as a result.

"Our customer was so upset; we were on the verge of losing the account. Your phone call calmed the customer's feelings and saved the day. Bravo."

Exactly How Did They Do It?

"I loved it, Leonor. You didn't reluctantly agree to do this. You said it with so much positive energy that it inspired all of us."

"Isaac, I appreciate what you did but also that you did it so thoroughly. You made sure to double-check every detail so that it was perfect when it went out the door. That's exceptional. Thank you."

This approach is useful because it requires that we be more mindful of the subtle details of how people acted, not just what they accomplished. Sometimes it helps to contrast the way they did it with how most people would have done it. Ask yourself, what would most people have done? What would most people have said?

"Many people these days don't seem to worry about the details. You do, and it made a world of difference here. Thanks."

Sometimes you can add extract impact to your praise by contrasting what they did with how you usually behave in comparable situations.

"Leonor, you expressed that so much more compassionately than I usually do. You phrased it in such a way that Bill got the message, but his feelings weren't hurt in the process. I have a lot to learn from you in that arena."

"You were so tactful in explaining things to Gene. I overheard how diplomatically you explained for the third time why we do the safety checks in the sequence we do. I have a tendency to be too blunt in giving feedback to people."

Are There Many People Who Would Do This Kind of Thing?

Another way to personalize praise is to be explicit about how uncommon their actions are.

"Thanks, Leonor. In these times of increased demands on all of us, there aren't many people who are willing to take on the added work of a beta test."

"Isaac, you're a rarity. So few people these days are willing to share the knowledge they've learned over years and years with an outsider, especially when the new person is their boss."

You have to be careful with this version of personalization so that it doesn't sound as though you're denigrating other people at the same time you're elevating this individual.

What Kind of Effort Did It Take?

"I know this required more work for you and your team. I'm so impressed that you're willing to make this sacrifice for the organization."

"I know that spending all this time teaching Gene means that you have to put in extra time to keep up with your regular work. That's really something, because I also know that's time that impacts your family as well."

Even if the person denies that it required more work, persist with your praise and watch how they react.

"Leonor, you're saying it's nothing and just part of your job, but I know you've had to come in the last two Saturdays."

When you persist by noting their special efforts, they'll usually own up to the extra work. My prediction is that Leonor will say something such as "And I came in last Sunday too." Her added description of the work she did provides another opportunity for you to praise those efforts as well.

What Do Their Actions Say About Them as People?

"Leonor, I always knew you were a special person, but this shows me how unique you are. Taking on this extra work demonstrates that you are a true team player."

"Isaac, you're quite a man. It takes a very big person to teach his own boss how to do his job."

What Will It Mean to Them in the Future?

This version must be used with caution, but it can be very effective with some types of employees. You must use care with your exact wording because you don't want to even hint that they'll receive a future substantive reward. In fact, it's useful to state clearly that you're not making any explicit promises. Reserve this approach to personalizing praise for people who are new to a position. Perhaps they were recently hired or were just promoted. They're grateful to be where they are and don't have any plans of immediate advancement or salary increase.

"That fact that you are a team player means there will be other opportunities for you to assume a leadership position. I don't know what form that will take. But lots of people are going to notice you because of this."

Or "I'm not making any promises; it's just that my experience is that the kind of effort you've made will serve you well over time in this organization or elsewhere."

It may be helpful to manage expectations explicitly about the relationship between praise and money. One way to avoid a misinterpretation is to make a general statement occasionally about your views of the relationship between praising and giving tangible rewards.

For instance, one manager did this by pointing out, "Although the word 'praise' contains the word 'raise,' there is a big difference between the two." About twice a year, she'd tell her people that many things are worthy of praise, but that doesn't mean they result in a raise. She would add, "Many praiseworthy things are more important and valuable in the long run than the things that produce raises. Because they are so valuable and so often go unnoticed, I like to take the time to acknowledge their significance with a few words of praise. In the same way, the words of praise you give a teammate are often more personally meaningful in the long run than money."

While caution is required, it's possible to make a general reference to the fact that good things happen to people who manifest such traits. While it's always good to err on the side of caution and explain that you aren't promising anything specifically, most people understand that you are making a general statement, not a specific commitment.

What Does It Say about Their Organization?

You can use this with someone from another business unit or from a different organization.

"The speed with which you responded to my problem tells me that Toyota really is concerned about customer satisfaction."

"When someone asks the location of a product, every employee in the store takes the customer to the exact aisle location. That only happens because you train your frontline partners as thoroughly as the Ritz Carlton trains its people."

Take the Time to Praise

When giving personalized praise, the exact words you say aren't critical. The real value of the words is based on the other person's knowledge that you have spent time thinking about him or her and took the time to express your thoughts and feelings. The message they will retain is that this manager really cares about me.

Truthfully, most of us don't bother to praise people because our attention is focused on two other things: our problems and ourselves. We're so busy looking for credit ourselves or trying to avoid personal blame and responsibility for a shortcoming that we don't really pay attention to what others are doing. As a result we often overlook the important little things they're doing to support us.

Some of us love to have problems. As soon as one crisis is solved, some managers go looking for the next one. They don't take time to recognize and celebrate the contribution of others. And if they can't find a new crisis, they'll elevate a standing issue to crisis status. They'll say something like, "The fact that we solved this problem temporarily doesn't mean everything is under control. We still have to worry about the Ajax account, so don't let this success go to your head." Facing a crisis gives them a sense of purpose and makes them feel important and needed.

Learning to praise effectively is one element that distinguishes a leader from a manager. Sometimes those who stay at the level of manager are so eager to be praised themselves that they seldom praise others. Their attention is self-focused and they see praising as a zero-sum game. Praising others' achievements, they seem to think, will diminish their own.

Real leaders, while still taking pride in their own accomplishments, operate at a more encompassing level. They see their job as creating an environment in which others can achieve outstanding results. Leaders know that bringing out the best in people means constantly recognizing their achievements.

Sometimes praising can be a challenge because there isn't much to praise. For instance, the worker may have tried the new approach once or twice but hasn't been successful. In essence they haven't yet accomplished anything you can pinpoint in your praise. In these instances, praise them for trying. You can acknowledge how much effort they put into the attempt or remark on how much it means to you that they are willing to try and keep trying.

The other secret to increasing the impact of your praise is to put it in writing. It doesn't have to be long, but just a sentence on paper can work wonders. Something as simple as "great job—thanks for all your efforts" can carry extra weight when it's a handwritten note from the boss. Most of us have a letter or note like that tucked away in a drawer or special location.

PERSONALIZING YOUR PRAISE UPWARD

It isn't just the people in the front lines who are stressed and worried during the initial stages of a change. Leaders have their doubts and fears just like everyone else. Whether you are their boss or their subordinate, a brief word of praise (not so much that it feels patronizing or ingratiatory) can give a leader added courage (the root of the word *encourage*) to take on the challenges of an implementation. Too often we forget, especially with more senior people, to say a few simple words of encouragement at the outset:

"You're the best person to lead this initiative."
"You've achieved so many things; I know you can do this too."
"It's going to be a pleasure to watch you take on this next challenge and to see how you turn it into a positive for everyone concerned."
"You can do it, and we're with you all the way."
"I have complete confidence in your ability to handle this."

Offering Tangible Rewards

Tangible rewards, such as monetary rewards, gift vouchers, and meals are important, and they must be dealt out carefully. At the very beginning of a change, intangibles have special importance. Initially your goal is to get employees just to try the new way and to keep making the effort, regardless of whether they are successful. Knowing that someone notices and cares is especially important at the start.

Tangible rewards, on the other hand, should be reserved for actual achievement. You can set achievable but challenging benchmarks along the path of change. These are the milestones that mark progress in Stages 2 and 3. Some managers prefer to set some easy benchmarks to guarantee "quick wins" as evidence of progress and to motivate further action. While there will be larger benchmarks to come in Stages 4 and 5, you want to be able to celebrate plenty of the little victories in the early stages.

When individuals or teams meet these smaller goals, you can supplement your words of praise with more tangible rewards. These need to be suited to the level of achievement. Some successes may deserve to be noted with some kind of substantive rewards. A free pizza lunch, for instance, or bagels at the morning break can be a great reward for a team as well as provide a forum for you to recognize the achievements to date and point people toward the next level.

For a change to be completed successfully through Stage 5 and to become the new way we do things, the formal reward system (such as compensation, bonuses, and promotions) has to be aligned with the change. In larger strategic terms, these more substantial rewards are vitally important to the successful institutionalization of the change. It is the responsibility of senior leaders to make certain the formal reward system recognizes people who are operating in the new system.

While the formal reward system is critical in the larger scheme of organizational change, all managers, high and low level, need to remember that praise is their most potent resource in the early stages of a change. Their personal involvement and their personalized words of recognition of other people's achievements are crucial in Stages 2 and 3.

Words of praise have several practical advantages. They're inexpensive and they are inside your realm of control. Middle managers seldom have much influence over the formal reward system, but informal rewards are totally in your control. Research shows that these informal rewards (e.g., recognition by a superior, a teammate's praise, the respect of colleagues) are much more important in driving everyday behavior than the distant, formal rewards.

Changing Your Praise Habits

Start small. Pick out one employee you have neglected to recognize and rehearse the words you want to use to personalize your praise. Look over the questions at the beginning of this chapter to decide exactly how you want to word your praise. As a next progressive step, you might want to go back to someone you've already praised in 40,000-foot generalities and now spell out your praise in ground-level personalized terms.

Another approach is to set a goal of doubling or tripling how much praise you give each week. You'll need to keep a rough count so you can gauge your progress. Deciding to give personalized praise to each person on your team once a week or once a month is easy to measure and to accomplish.

Regardless of how you define your new praise goals, it's important to begin. Do it today and keep doing it. Before you know it, you'll be in Stage 4 in this personal J Curve of changing another aspect of your management style. You'll become a convert to praising when you see your expressions of appreciation reciprocated in the words and faces of your teammates.

Chapter

8

MAKE IT EASY TO START

If you're like a lot of seasoned managers, at some time in your career you've probably applied for a job that was beyond your experience or education. During the selection process you were confident you could do the job. After all, it basically came down to managing people and you knew you were great at that. You also knew you were a quick study and figured you could learn the ins and outs of the larger responsibilities that came with the job. Sure enough, your boss picked you.

If not the first day, then invariably on the second or the third, you came home thinking you had made a horrible mistake. This job requires much more than you imagined. The same thoughts kept circling in your mind. "I'll never master this.... I'm bound to fail.... How could I have ever dreamed I was capable of this level of management?... I have no idea how to make this work."

The next morning you happen to run into the boss, who cheerfully inquires how things are going. Because you're so full of self-doubt, you admit that you're having a few challenges. He just keeps smiling and launches into a pep talk. "Don't think like that. Get a hold of yourself. You're good. You're really good. You're the perfect person for this position. I have no doubts about your ability to succeed. Go get 'em, tiger. You can do it."

As he walks away, how do you feel? For a minute or two, his words of praise and confidence raise your spirits. Then, as you walk toward your office, you realize he didn't want to hear your fears. You still have them, and you don't have concrete solutions to the problems you face.

Your boss was trying to help you deal with your feelings of self-doubt in the best way he knew—communicating his confidence in you. While it's great to know that your superiors believe in you, that's usually not what we need to help us keep going through that chasm of terror. Activation supplements these words of encouragement with specific tools that make it easy for people to get started taking on the challenges of Stage 2.

In this chapter you'll learn a set of practical skills you can use to make it comfortable for your team to get out of their comfort zones and take those first difficult steps.

SYMPATHIZING WITH NEGATIVE REACTIONS

During the challenging initial stages of a change, you will often hear people say:

"This is too hard."
"I hate doing this."
"Who thought up this crazy idea?"
"The old way is so much better."
"We'll never make this work."

Have you noticed how most managers react to this kind of complaining? They don't like it, and they say so in no uncertain terms. For example:

"I don't want to hear any whining."
"No negativity. This is the way things are, so just accept it."
"You should be glad you have a job."
"You're acting like a bunch of babies. Quit crying, and just do what you're told."
"If you don't like the way things are around here, then leave."

Many managers feel they need to stifle all complaints. They react defensively because they perceive employees' laments as a personal attack on themselves and their decision to make this change. They feel the need to squelch all dissent because they're afraid that it will get others complaining and the whole initiative will bog down.

Actually, it's perfectly normal for people to complain when they run into problems while doing a task they don't like and didn't choose. Think about a personal example in your own life. Let's say that despite your protests, someone drags you to an event. In route you encounter traffic congestion, parking is a problem, long lines greet you at the ticket windows, and you end up with poor seats. For some of us, this might occur when we're forced to go to an opera; for others, it might be a NASCAR race. Most of us would whine and moan at each obstacle along the way and probably voice our desire to be at home. We'd think our complaints were perfectly reasonable.

In the same way, it's reasonable for employees to express negative feelings about an unwanted change when they make mistakes and have setbacks during Stages 2 and 3. Their complaints don't necessarily mean that they're going to stop moving forward. It's just that they're frustrated at this moment and want to express it.

In the previous personal example, what do you want to hear when you're whining and complaining? Your first choice might be "Okay, we don't have to go to the opera (race)." Even if you can't escape the anticipated torture, you'd at least like someone to sympathize with you, someone who will say:

"Yes, this traffic congestion is frustrating."
"Parking really is a challenge."
"The ticketing process is a mess."
"At times like this, staying at home does have its appeals."

If we must do something distasteful, we like people to acknowledge our unhappy feelings and the sacrifices we're making. The truth is we're all like children who seek sympathy and comfort when we cry out. We don't want to be told to shut up. We resent it when people tell us to just be patient because we're going to like NASCAR or the opera (as we ultimately may). And it can really make our blood boil to be told we're acting like a child, even though we know we are.

By being aware of how much you like it when people sympathize with your complaints should make it easier for you to acknowledge other people's complaints. Sincerely showing sympathy doesn't mean you have to turn into a junior psychologist or touchy-feely talk-show host. It means simply acknowledging the other person's right to express some negative feelings. An easy way to start doing that is to employ what I call *the bamboo technique*.

When a strong wind comes, the bamboo bends and then it snaps back. So the bamboo technique also has two parts—bending and snapping back. Bending involves acknowledging the other person's feelings. Watch how it can be applied to some of the common complaints during a change.

When they say, "This is too hard," you can say, "Yes, these first stages of implementation really are hard."
If they say, "I hate doing this," you can respond, "I can see that you really hate this new approach."

If they utter, "We'll never make this work," you can bend by saying, "You may be right that it's going to be challenging to make this work."

When they opine, "The old way was so much better," you can reply, "The old way did have some advantages."

Even if they attack you personally, as in "Who thought up this crazy idea?" you can say, "This was another of my crazy ideas—some of them work and some don't."

Often you can acknowledge their complaints by using their same language (e.g., too hard...hate it...crazy, and so on) in a phrase that shows that you heard what they said and it has some legitimacy (e.g., yes, it is hard...some of my ideas *are* crazy...the old way did have many good features). In some cases, you might even express qualified agreement with what they said, for example, "You could be right. We may never make this work."

The second aspect of the bamboo technique is to bend back. In the context of implementation, this means describing the actions the person should try next. After bending, you could use statements such as these:

"If you just do it a few more times, I think you'll get it."

"Keep doing what you just did and I think it will work for you."

"Let's try again with a little more energy and enthusiasm."

By sincerely acknowledging the worker's complaints in the bending portion of the bamboo technique, you let them know that you know how they feel and that you are concerned about them. When you snap back with concrete action recommendations, you get them refocused on taking doable action in the new direction. Ideally, they will experience success on their next attempt. If they don't, you'll need to keep urging and encouraging until they do succeed with the new approach.

Instead of using the bamboo technique, many managers respond to these kinds of complaints with personal criticism, name-calling, and other forms of defensiveness. This can divert both the manager and the employee. The employee will respond to the manager's criticism with criticism of his own, and soon a brouhaha erupts. Progress halts during the altercation, and untangling the mess will delay the change even longer.

We get caught in our defensive reactions because we fear that if we give any credence to employees' complaints, they will use that as proof that they can stop trying to work on the implementation. Experience shows that most mature people won't simply stop because of one setback or even a string of frustrations. They just want to complain about the parts they don't like.

Usually, they just want to assert their right to complain and to know that the boss has honestly listened to them. Voicing their unhappiness and having it acknowledged, they'll get back to the work at hand. By being positive and specific about what they should do next, managers can help people get reengaged with the task at hand.

The bamboo technique can also be useful when you are first presenting a new initiative. If employees raise specious objections, you can use the bamboo technique to deflect their protests. Naturally, if they are voicing a legitimate concern, you'll want to adapt your plan to handle their objection. Here are some examples.

When someone complains that your new initiative is another example of spending too much money on marketing gimmicks rather than investing in production equipment, you can say, "It's always difficult to balance the money we spend on marketing and production, and I need to keep that in mind. In this case, we are committed to implementing this new initiative, and the way people can help make it a success is by..."

In the same way, imagine someone who attacks you personally as a way of getting you to back away from making them implement a new plan. You might use the bamboo technique by saying something like,

"You're right. We MBAs do come up with some harebrained ideas. In this case, however, I'm absolutely convinced this is a good idea, and I'm asking for everyone's support. Here is what we need to do to make this a reality. . . ."

You begin by sincerely acknowledging there may be value in what they are saying, but after bending, you refocus on the actions they need to take in the new direction. Again, this is only used with objections you judge to be resistance. If someone raises a legitimate concern, you obviously want to think it through and revise your plans in light of their constructive suggestions.

CREATING A SAFE LEARNING ENVIRONMENT

A motivational slogan asks, "What would you do in life if you knew you couldn't fail?" Most of us can quickly identify many things we've avoided because of concerns about failure. Your internal voice of fear may sound like this:

"What will people think of me?"
"I'll look like a fool."
"I could hurt myself."
"I'm too old (young) to do that."

By listening to those voices, we often remain wedded to our established patterns and routines.

The people you're leading through this exciting new change are hearing those kinds of voices too. Their big fear is how you, their boss, will react to their failures. Their worries are so great that it stops some of them from even trying. If you remove the basis for such fears, it's amazing what people are willing to try.

Let's bring this recommendation down to ground level. How do you make employees feel safe making mistakes as they learn something completely new? What could you say to make them feel comfortable going over that emotional cliff?

Because they're so accustomed to management getting angry and punitive when someone makes a mistake, employees don't really believe you when you say it's okay to make errors at the beginning. Don't take this mistrust personally. It's based on their past experiences, which began long before you came into the picture.

Although you can give them verbal reassurances, there's only one thing that will truly help them begin to trust your words: how you react when someone makes a mistake. And not just the first mistake, but the second and third time as well. Everyone will be watching whether you criticize or applaud when people make errors. That's right—applaud. The alternative to criticism is praise, not merely remaining silent and saying nothing.

To help people trust your words, you must virtually celebrate their missteps. You can say things such as:

"That's okay. I'm so glad you tried. Now try it again."

"Good for you. The only way we're going to get better is by being brave enough to try and try again."

"Thanks for having the courage to try and keep on trying."

"Bravo! That was a glorious failure because we can use it to learn and improve."

"The only mistake we can make is not to make mistakes. We have to try and fail again and again before we can make this work."

Obviously, you're not going to be urging people to make mistakes that could produce disastrous consequences. You don't want employees jeopardizing an important client relationship or a major product run as part of the early stages of learning. Instead, you can create a safe practice environment or a low-risk simulation for them to begin. If they've received good skills training, most people can quickly "go live" with some real, but small-scale, pilots. A salesperson, for example, might try the new approach with a trusted customer who has been alerted that this is a trial run.

PROVIDE PRACTICAL EDUCATION

People do want to understand where the change is headed, why the organization needs to go there, and what the benefits will be once it gets there. But more important, they need to understand *how* they are going to be able to get there. Education and training before and during execution must emphasize detailed knowledge of how to do things the new way.

People need some realistic opportunities to practice. "Learning by doing" needs to be a part of all classroom teaching, coaching, books, or online courses. The formula is pretty simple: short education segments, followed by a chance to practice; feedback about performance; refined practice; and then restart the cycle on the next lesson.

Individual coaching is labor-intensive but can also yield big results quickly. In addition to hiring outside experts to do the coaching, consider inside coaches. For instance, if another division or department has already successfully implemented the change, perhaps some of those associates could coach your people. You also probably have some people on your team who are already well into Stage 4 or 5. You can use them too, *if* they're good teachers. That's an important qualification. In front of colleagues, many "experts" like parading their skills rather than sharing them. If you can coach your more advanced people on how to coach, they can be a low-cost source of education.

In many cases, you don't have to find a team member who has completely mastered the new approach. All you need is a good coach who is a few steps ahead of the individual he's helping. Include yourself in the list of coaches. Then, do some of the coaching yourself. It's a safe bet that you'll learn as much as you teach. The time you spend helping your key managers, or frontline people, will help you learn what the change really means to those down in the trenches. As you experience their fears and frustrations, you'll be more sympathetic with their plight.

You'll have a stronger sense of gratitude for their sacrifices, and your praise will be more heartfelt.

OFFER SAFETY IN NUMBERS

It's easier to take on a seemingly overwhelming challenge if you have others around. For those who are afraid of going over the emotional cliff, having a buddy, or a whole team of buddies, can make it much less frightening. There's something about knowing that other people truly understand your pain that decreases how much it hurts.

In each step from the initial training to the actual launch, it's smart to have work peers offer advice and give pep talks. Teammates who share common frustrations and doubts are also exceptionally good at offering sympathetic support. They know almost exactly what the rank and file are feeling and can put those feelings into words that are much more meaningful than the usual canned presentation from the trainer sent out from headquarters.

A major change has a wide impact on many people, even in small- and medium-sized organizations, so it's usually not difficult to find coworkers undergoing similar challenges. People who are separated physically or psychologically may require special efforts. That person could be an outside salesperson, for example, who works from home and is always traveling. Or it could be the only person who handles internal auditing, on whom the new financial software would have a unique impact.

You'll need to create ways these employees can have frequent and open communication with coworkers going through the same change. Make sure they talk to one another by phone regularly. In one department, a paired buddy system was created in which employees were required to talk to one another every day for at least 15 minutes. A simple outline was prepared daily so that it was easy for them to cover the important issues.

In another instance, coworkers in different national regions had a weekly video conference in which they shared doubts, concerns, and encouragement. An agenda of topics was sent out, and everyone was required to talk about what was going poorly as well as the things that were going according to plan. These kinds of far-flung employees need more than an occasional e-mail inquiry or a brief call from a disinterested boss ("You're not having any problems out there in Wheeling, are you?").

One exception to the safety-in-numbers wisdom involves individuals who are very sensitive to the prospect of letting others see them fail. Because they want to project an image of knowing everything, they'll resist any change that might reveal their fallibility. Their pride, misplaced as it may be, becomes a huge barrier to trying something new. I've seen this occur with senior executives, prima donna salespeople, an engineer with a degree from Cal Tech and an ego from Texas, and long-time supervisors who try to act as if they've seen it all and can do anything.

For those who have painted themselves into this kind of a change-inhibiting box, you may need to provide private instruction. If the person is crucial to the success of the initiative, it may be worth spending the extra resources to provide individual coaching or a learning environment that is not only safe but also secure from peeking eyes.

In the case of one top salesperson, the coaching didn't even deal with how to use the new approach and materials. He understood that almost immediately. His resistance came from an unwillingness to publicly admit to the other salespeople that he was actually changing his approach to selling. The coach helped him find a way to save face. Together they came up with a rationale that was used to explain to his colleagues that he had really been incorporating key elements of the "new" technique into the approach he had been using for years.

GIVING WORDS OF ENCOURAGEMENT

Simple, supportive words can also create a positive impetus for change, but they often work differently than we think.

"You can do it."
"Remember how well you did on the last software conversion."
"Hey, you're numero uno; you can do anything."

These kinds of encouraging phrases are virtual platitudes and are often treated as such by people who are frightened. When people become debilitated by their fear, they discount the actual content of what you're saying. In fact, while you're talking they may be privately rebutting what you are saying, such as:

"No, I can't do it. I have no idea how to do it."
"This is different. The last time was hard, but this is impossible."
"Right. I'm number one. Number one fool. No, I'm number zero."

We believe we're boosting their morale by making them feel good about themselves so that they'll tackle the change. Only rarely do our words themselves make people feel better. Paradoxically, even though our positive statements may not increase confidence, they may actually increase the chances that the person will start down the new path. Your encouraging words send an important implicit message. "I expect you to do this and will be disappointed if you don't."

This subliminal pressure can induce people to at least make a few attempts at doing things the new way. For this reason alone, it's worth giving people personal words of support as they begin Stage 2.

Ideally, they'll have success on their first few tries. Even if they don't, they'll at least discover that the "monsters" aren't so ferocious. This reduced level of fear means that some of the other activation techniques you are using will get them to keep trying a few more times.

HELP THEM GET STARTED

"Try it. You'll see it's not that hard. You'll like it, and it's going to make your work easier. It's really not that difficult. It's going to be better for all of us. Besides you're good at this kind of thing. Just get your courage up and do it."

Leaders often resort to these kinds of exhortations. For the leader, the change isn't that big a deal, perhaps because he's already in Stage 5. He knows the change is going to produce good results, so he keeps urging people to start doing it. When employees argue and drag their feet, leaders may get louder and more insistent. Resistance and frustration quickly reach the boiling point. Instead of trying to push people over the emotional cliff, concentrate on making it easy for people to take the first steps.

Make It Easy to Start

For example, rather than wasting time repeatedly by exhorting the call-center staff to cross-sell other products, you could use that time to write a rough script of things those salespeople could say. Giving this kind of concrete assistance produces better results for several reasons. First, you've taken a moderately high-altitude phrase "cross-sell other products" down to ground level for them. And if you involve them in writing the script, they'll have a greater commitment to using it. Plus the time you've invested tells them how serious you are about expecting them to achieve this new goal.

The heavy lifting of execution takes place in the first half of the J Curve, so you should begin providing assistance in Stage 1 where people are still thinking about whether they can successfully make the change. By defining the first actions in simple terms, you switch employees' focus from the future to the present and make the change seem much more doable.

Helping employees spell out their first steps may sound as though it will take more of your time than you'd like. Initially it could, but it's far better than the usual alternative. Most managers see persuasion as a low-cost answer to the challenges of getting people to do things differently. They think that making a direct request, backed by logic—even if they have to repeat it over and over—is the quickest way to get people to change. When persuasion doesn't work, managers voice their frustration. "Why don't they just do what I tell them to do?"

I'm sure you realize by now that the prior paragraphs are an attempt to "persuade" you to use the activation technique of making it easy to get started with the new change. As such, these paragraphs contradict the wisdom of activation. So, in addition to reading about taking action, I need to make it easy for *you* to get started.

Pick out one employee on your team and one small change you'd like her to make. If no one comes to mind, go back to Chapter 5 on ground-level communication. Remember one change goal that you were working on and spell it out down in the dirt. Whom would you like to get working on that goal?

Once you've identified a specific person, think about anything that person might consider to be an impediment to starting. You need to think from the other person's perspective. What might she see as potential obstacles, no matter how tiny? Better still, get the person to talk about what would make it hard for her to get started in the new direction.

Think of ways you could assist by removing the obstacles and breaking the change into ground-level steps. If, for example, you want this person to begin calling old customers to tell them about your new services, you might take 10 minutes to brainstorm about which 20 old customers she could call. Those few minutes can make it so much easier for her to get started. Yes, it would be even easier if you helped look up the phone numbers for all 20, and maybe you'd be willing to do that as well.

Providing scripts, checklists, and explicit guidelines may make you feel as though you're babying people and not respecting them as adults.

That would be true if you were writing out such detailed prescriptions for already motivated professionals. But you're dealing with employees who are wrestling with a series of emotional roadblocks, and all they can think about are the dire consequences they imagine will result from going down this new path.

When employees are paralyzed by fear, they need very specific and explicit directions on how to begin. Because they're partially immobilized, they'll perceive your assistance as coming from a true partner who really cares, not from a micromanager.

Here's another example. At first Miguel refused the offer of a new job assignment that would require him to make driving trips outside the office several times a day. His manager really wanted Miguel to take this assignment but said she'd respect his decision. Wisely, she probed for the reasons Miguel didn't want the assignment. The answer was that the new job sounded as though he'd be overwhelmed with information about where to go, how to get there, whom he was to see, and what he was to accomplish. Almost as a joking aside, Miguel said, "I'd need a personal digital assistant to keep track of all that information." The manager quickly said she'd provide a beeper, cell phone, and the personal assistant. And just as quickly, Miguel said he'd give the job a try.

Providing new equipment, furniture, an office, or even helping temporarily with childcare may be good investments if it helps key people start down the path of change. Similarly, providing extensive group training, buttressed with personal coaches, may be a very smart approach. The money you spend greasing the start of the new track will be repaid by the increased speed with which employees head toward the finish.

Raise the Bar

Receiving praise—and lots of it—at the beginning of a change makes it so much easier for employees to keep trying to learn a new skill. When all you seem to be doing is failing, it's nice to hear something positive.

As a manager one of your main responsibilities is to praise your employees. Initially, you'll be praising them for any little step in the right direction. The fact that they even tried is worthy of sincere applause.

Once they've had two or three successes, gradually raise the standard a little higher. Don't rush this process. Keep the new goal within reach. They may need you to help them discover ways they can go farther and farther. As you raise the performance bar, you no longer praise them for merely trying; now they must achieve at an advanced level to win your accolades.

A bar can be raised in many ways. It may just be that the employees must master more and more sections of the training manual or program. In other cases, they may need to begin practicing using the new approach with more complicated cases. Or it could be that they have to increase their speed or reduce their error rate. Sympathetically and clearly, communicate your expectation that they should be successively doing more.

"That was great. You've got the basics. Let's see if you can do it in under five minutes this time."

"I think you're getting there. You were great with an in-house customer. Now try it with an external customer."

Beg, Bargain, and Bribe

Despite using all the activation tools, there will be times when you still won't be able to get a Resister to take the first few steps off the emotional cliff. No matter how easy you make it, he or she won't budge.

When all else has failed, you'll have to find extra incentives. You are reduced to the three Bs: begging, bargaining, and bribing.

"Please, as a personal favor to me, just do it a couple times, will you?"

"This is critically important, and I really, really need your help on this one."

"I'll get down on bended knee if that's what it takes to get you to start using the new procedure."

"Humor me this time. Just give it a try."

Although begging may be personally distasteful, it could be a relatively low-cost way to get employees to take the first few steps in the new direction. Reserve the three Bs for really important Resisters, such as those who can influence others. Make sure they're going to experience some degree of success almost immediately. Count on those quick successes to motivate the Resisters and turn them into believers.

Despite feeling humiliated and resentful at having to plead, you may encounter last-ditch situations in which you must do it. Your only leverage with important Resisters may be to beg them to do what you're asking. While they wouldn't readily admit it in public, many change leaders regularly resort to some form of groveling to get key people to go along with the plan.

Of course, if it's really important for you to get the other person to get on board, he'll probably be smart enough to raise his price. Your begging is a sign that he's got something you really need, so he'll try to get you to give him even more in return for his support. Now it becomes a negotiation. He gives you his endorsement of the change—and the backing of those over whom he has influence—if you will do something for him. Exactly what he wants becomes the make-or-break question. In such situations, hold off on telling him what you'd be willing to do for his support. It's better to start by asking questions, like these:

"What could I do to get you to take these steps to make this happen?"

"What would it take to get your support?"

"I'd be very grateful for your backing. How could I show my gratitude?"

"Is there anything I could do, anything at all that could get you to do this?"

Asking what he wants before telling him what you would do can save a lot of wasted time and expense. You'll sometimes be very wrong in your predictions about what the other person wants. By asking up front, you find out exactly what the stakes are. That can save the time of backtracking through your proposal to learn what the person is really after. Also, you may be underestimating the value he puts on things you could do for him. He may ask you to do something that really isn't that costly to you.

Employees skilled in these kinds of negotiations will often throw your questions right back at you with a question of their own:

"What do you have to offer?"
"Exactly what would you be willing to do for me?"

They're trying to reverse the dynamic and get you to go first in indicating how much you'd be willing to pay before they tell you how much they'd be willing to take. With practice you can learn to bounce this question right back to them, such as "Well, that depends. I'm sure not going to do anything unethical or illegal, but maybe we can find a way to work together. What do you have in mind that would make this work for you?"

Remember that this is a two-way process. In addition to knowing what they want from you, it's vitally important that you know exactly what you want from them. This is no time for 40,000-foot generalities. Because you must seal this deal in ground-level terms, take time to practice putting your request into words.

"If you'll sign your name to the announcement, attend the kick-off program, and make sure that all your team leaders begin using the new software package and that they will disable the old system, then I'd be willing to...."

"If you'll attend the three-hour training session, obtaining a score of 80 percent, and then actually use the new procedure for two days, then I'd be happy to...."

These are meant as generic illustrations. You will be able to get even more specific in real life. With your knowledge of the employee and the specifics of your work situation, you should be able to tell him exactly what he'll need to agree to do if a bargain is to be achieved.

We've been discussing the bargaining process, but bribery (the informal, not the illegal kind) isn't that different. In both cases you are offering to give something to the other person if he or she will do something for you in return. We usually consider it a bribe when the value of what is being asked for is outrageously costly, unethical, or completely undeserved.

It's hard to imagine someone so important that you would ever violate your ethics. But a particular change initiative may develop in which you would be willing to give a high-ranking, or influential, individual things he considers valuable to get him to publicly buy in to the change. Be careful, though. This is a slippery slope, and you could end up having to pay an even higher price in the future, especially if he tells people what you did for him. If you are sure you can do it once and not persist, then the benefits may outweigh the costs in just this one case.

So far we've been talking about using make-it-easy-to-start methods with subordinates facing change. But higher-ups, too, can fear the unknown and sometimes you can use these methods with them as well. An important part of managing up involves making it easy for your superiors to begin doing things differently.

For instance, I recall a situation in which a team was celebrating a small but significant milestone along the path of change. The team leader had the idea of having the regional manager stop by and express her pleasure at their achievement. He knew this would really energize the group. The regional manager was only in this location once a month, and her schedule was filled with meetings that were supposedly far more important than the celebration of one team's victory. He guessed she'd want to help celebrate but that it might be hard to get her to actually stop by.

The team leader thought: What objections might she raise?

"It will take too long."
"I don't know when I'd have time during the day because my schedule is always changing."
"I'm not even sure I know how to get to the room where you're holding the celebration. Besides, what would I say if I did come?"
"How long do I actually have to be there?"

Here's how the team leader decided to respond. "It would be great if you could stay for five or ten minutes, but we'd be overjoyed with two minutes. We'll be completely flexible and will arrange the celebration for a time that fits your schedule. Let's plan a tentative time and if your schedule changes, we'll readjust the time of the event to fit. We can organize the group on short notice because, after all, we specialize in quick changes. Give us a ten-minute warning, and we'll get the team assembled. Irene will come to your location and guide you to the break room. Actually, Irene made a key contribution to our success. She'd love to walk you over. Your remarks can be very brief. Here's a list of a few talking points I've heard you discuss in the past. If you could mention any or all of these things, it would mean the world to our team. At what time could we tentatively schedule your appearance?"

With a little planning and extra effort, most or all of the barriers the other person puts up can be minimized or eliminated so that it's easy for her to do what you want. When asked directly, many employees—whatever their rank—will tell you what you could do to help them get started, so just ask:

"What could I do to…

make it easy for you to try this?"
reduce the amount of work involved in initiating this change?"
remove obstacles that make it hard for you to try this new approach?"
make it less frightening to experiment with this new situation?"
support you in beginning this transition?"

Employees are usually willing to tell you exactly what would make it painless for them, and often their answers are surprising, such as:

"You could get someone else to finish the clerical parts of the Ajax project, so that I had time to work on the new initiative."

"If I had that new software package, it would be a lot easier for me to tackle this thing."

"Let me try it in private on my own, without a lot of people watching me."

"If you hired a personal coach or trainer to help me get started, I'd be willing to do it."

"Send me to that week-long training program in Hawaii."

The fact that employees want some form of assistance doesn't mean you'll necessarily provide it. Obviously, you have to assess the cost and whether it's worth the investment. Often, it's well worth the expense to provide some added resources just to get the person to agree to actually try doing things the new way. In the final analysis, it's the impact of your persistent interest, encouragement, and confidence that will carry the day. Knowing you are personally invested in helping them change will serve as the most potent incentive to action.

SECTION

3

SUSTAINING CHANGE

Chapter

9

ASSIGN ACCOUNTABILITY

Only when you sustain the changes you've worked so hard to implement do you reap the long-term benefits of your efforts. Maintenance of a change so that it becomes a part of everyday work life isn't as demanding as instituting the change, but it requires that managers learn certain skills. Foremost among these is creating a culture of accountability to turn the "new" way into standard operating procedure. You also want to create an enthusiastic environment that continues to promote innovation and change.

Establishing accountability and encouraging change are necessary during implementation as well as during the maintenance phase of change. These two topics will be discussed in the next two chapters. We'll begin with concrete ways you can get both the courage and the skills to hold people accountable.

CREATING ACCOUNTABILITY

Peg has a pet peeve. She dislikes dirt and disorder. She wants *everything* to be spotless and orderly. Everyone at work puts up with her compulsive tendency because she is a great leader and has compiled an outstanding record as a general manager.

As a result, public areas in her department are immaculate, offices and cubicles are uncluttered, desks are cleared at night, workers police themselves in the break rooms and even clean up after one another in the bathrooms. When new people are hired, what do you think they learn from coworkers their very first day on the job?

Peg gets virtually everyone, including the folks who are normally extremely disorganized, to keep things neat and clean. Much as we may dislike working for people who have a pet peeve, you have to admire their ability to get people to change their normal habits.

How do they do it? By holding people accountable. Peg clearly communicates her expectations, and she keeps repeating those desires. She monitors follow-through and notices those who make exceptional efforts at orderliness and sings their praises. She also spots those who remain messy and lets them know privately that they're not living up to expectations.

Peg's approach contains valuable lessons for all of us. We can use similar techniques to hold employees to their commitments to change. This chapter explains how you can create accountability by linking individuals' performance to achieve larger organizational goals.

Faulty implementation, not ill-conceived ideas, causes most change initiatives to fail. And a breakdown of accountability is a key contributor to this lack of success. Leaders fail to live up to their promises, and employees fail to live up to theirs. Action plans are never fully implemented so their benefits are never realized.

Accountability involves the real-world results of our actions—both acts of commission when we make errors and acts of omission when we fail to do what we promised. Holding people accountable means giving them rewards if they do what they committed to do and not rewarding them if they don't.

THE NECESSITY OF ACCOUNTABILITY

People resist changes that they think will be bad for them. They're especially likely to resist in Stage 2 when they are making mistakes and performing poorly. To escape from this disagreeable situation, they revert to the old way they've always done things. Accountability is critical at all stages of a change, but it's especially important at the beginning when people most want to avoid doing things the new way.

Think about change implementation as a three-legged stool. The first leg is specifying exactly what actions people should take—spelling it out at ground level. The second leg is rewarding people for taking those actions—front-loading. Essentially, activation is based on the "if—then" connection between behavior and rewards. *If* you take these actions, *then* you'll receive these rewards.

Accountability is the third leg of the stool, and it connects the "if" and "then" legs with three more words: if, *and only if*, then. It's necessary because, being human, we often try to find shortcuts to get the rewards without doing the required actions.

Leaders must make it clear what is expected of employees in implementing the change. They must explain the personal benefits to the workers if they make the change happen, as well as the negative personal consequences if they don't make it happen. These benefits may be tangible (e.g., financial bonuses) or intangible (e.g., feelings of pride and accomplishment). The negative consequences may involve remedial work, reassignment, or job reclassification. Any time a leader warns people of possible negative consequences, he or she should also emphasize that assistance will be available to help employees achieve the new goal.

What happens to a change initiative when the leader doesn't hold people accountable and tolerates resistance? Imagine the classic kick-off meeting to launch a new initiative. The chief executive officer (CEO) is at the podium, and seated beside him, two on each side, are the chief financial officer (CFO), the executive vice president (EVP) of marketing, the chief legal counsel, and the executive vice president of operations. As the CEO details the benefits of the new change, you notice the faces of his sidekicks on the stage. Three of them seem to be transfixed. The CFO is nodding her head in agreement. The marketing EVP is focused on the CEO as if hypnotized by the power of his words, and the attorney is smiling. But what is the old-timer from operations doing? With a scowl on his face, he's gently shaking his head in consternation.

What's your prediction? Mine is that if the head of operations doesn't favor the change, the key managers who report to him will immediately get the signal to resist it. And if operations isn't on board, what are the change's chances of success? In most companies, unless a change has the complete backing of all the key players, it's going to fail.

This holds true whether it's a CEO allowing a senior executive to resist or a supervisor who tolerates the resistance of a key member of a work team. Everyone can, and does, read between the lines of the Resister's behavior, that is, you don't really have to do this because other people aren't doing it, and nothing bad is happening to them. When employees get that message from a leader's inaction, you can say goodbye to morale, goodbye to any chance of implementing the change, goodbye to the leader's credibility and, probably shortly, goodbye to his career.

If the failure to strictly enforce accountability across the board undercuts a manager's ability to lead, why wouldn't he or she always hold employees accountable?

The most common reason is fear. The leader fears employees will dislike him and an emotional confrontation will result. If he really makes them angry, they may stop trying to implement the change. They could even rebel and sabotage his efforts. When paranoia is in full bloom, the leader may imagine key employees banding together to mutiny or at least to go over his head to higher authorities. To avoid such dissension, the leader allows some employees to continue working as before even though they didn't implement the change.

Sometimes leaders are just not prepared for the excuses that people come up with for the failure to implement a change. For example, "The machine broke and, according to the service contract, we could only use their authorized technicians. So we had to wait until they could work us into their schedule." Or the ever-popular "Pete is on vacation and he was the only one who had access to that information. He was on a fishing trip in Alaska for ten days and couldn't be contacted." Surprised by their seemingly reasonable justifications, the leader may excuse them—this time. But usually it's not just this time. There'll be a different excuse next time, plus other employees will notice the lapse in accountability and they'll be tempted to try it too.

In other cases, the leader may feel uncomfortable holding employees accountable because he didn't clearly spell out exactly what was expected of them at the beginning and didn't explicitly tell them of the negative consequences if they failed. Thinking that he didn't really give them specific directions and a clear warning in advance, he rationalizes that it isn't reasonable to hold them accountable "this time."

The usual reason leaders don't communicate those details is that they're afraid that placing such clear demands on an employee might make the worker angry, causing further trouble. So they only allude to goals and hint about consequences but never detail them completely. They hope the other person will get the unspecified message, but they also give him an out. Because the leaders didn't specify the details, he usually caves in when the unrepentant employee says, "But you didn't tell me exactly what we were supposed to do, and you never told me of these draconian punishments. You're not being fair."

Allowing people to escape accountability is especially likely to happen when the culprit is a friend, an influential individual, or a powerful manager. Your friend or someone who did a favor for you in the past will now call in his "chits" and assert that you cannot hold him accountable. The important manager makes the same plea: she had bigger concerns that interfered with her opportunity to learn how to use the new procedures. Of course, she promises to follow the new rules next time. Want to bet?

Most of us favor the idea of holding people responsible for their actions. Everybody, we believe, should be rewarded for successful actions, and negative consequences should befall everyone who fails to live up to their promises—everyone, *except ourselves and our close associates.* Our failures are different. Mitigating reasons explain and excuse why we failed; therefore, we shouldn't be blamed or punished. Making exceptions to accountability for yourself or your friends and allies is going to create precedents that will be disastrous.

Understanding these reasons why we avoid establishing and enforcing accountability provides some insights into how we should do it. The lessons we can take away from this analysis are that we need to find a way to reduce our fears, neutralize excuses in advance, make clear to employees exactly what is expected and what the positive and negative consequences will be.

ESTABLISHING ACCOUNTABILITY

How you bring up the topic of accountability will be important. If you are too strident about it, you'll sound as if you're more intent on punishment than progress. Treat it too lightly and employees will infer your heart isn't in it. So you can greatly lubricate the change mechanism by putting some thought into how you discuss accountability.

Here are seven elements of accountability that should be covered by managers at all levels as they explain a new change to their direct reports:

1. Mutually set performance expectations.
2. Specify performance agreements at ground level.

3. Specify the positive and negative consequences of performance.
4. Link performance to larger organizational goals.
5. Plan for problems.
6. Decide how to communicate progress.
7. Publicly commit to accountability.

Mutually Set Performance Expectations

It isn't just those in the field who have to be held accountable; the leaders do as well. Both managers and team members enter into a mutual agreement about what they'll do by what dates. Each party needs to make promises to one another and then live up to their promises.

Too often accountability is treated as a one-way obligation of the workers, with management telling them what they must do. Management must also perform. Typically, it must provide resources, information, training, communications, performance feedback, and coaching, as well as integrating and monitoring everyone's progress.

Involving all parties in designing and planning the way the change is to be executed provides a platform for discussing everyone's responsibilities. Involving people in designing the details of the implementation plan means each person will have a say, or at least an awareness, of what's expected of everyone. Making the expectations a mutual process motivates employees to live up to their commitments and gives them an incentive to monitor other people's progress. They feel more comfortable encouraging a coworker with statements such as "We both promised we were going to make this change happen, and I've been doing my part. But you haven't done your part yet. Come on, we need you."

Specify Performance Agreements at Ground Level

The core of accountability is spelling out behavioral contracts or action plans. Simple changes may not require a detailed, formal contract.

However, in complex situations, or ones in which people have not lived up to their past promises, the contract must be spelled out in greater detail and everyone should get a copy.

Whether the agreement is oral or written, this is the place for SMART goals: Specific, Measurable, Achievable, Realistic, and Timely. These agreements should specify:

- What goal each person or group will pursue and what results will be produced
- How they will go about achieving the goal
- Who will be primarily responsible for making sure it gets done
- When it will be done
- What resources will be used to do it
- How people will communicate progress with others
- The consequences of fulfilling, or not fulfilling, the agreement

It may seem tedious, or like micromanaging, to spell out all this detail, but experience shows that it's best if someone takes notes in any meeting where planning agreements are being worked out. The parties should write their agreement at the meeting or the notes should be circulated immediately after the meeting. When these minutes are sent out, they usually carry the proviso that unless someone disagrees, this document will stand as the formal agreement.

The specificity of the agreement also provides benchmarks for measuring progress. By linking a timeline to completing subgoals, it's possible to monitor everyone's progress. When parties fall behind, they have an obligation to communicate their problems to others. This can also be an opportunity to seek assistance in order to meet the time deadlines.

Specify the Consequences of Performance

At a conceptual level, accountability can be expressed as two "if . . . then" statements: *If* you achieve these results, *then* you will receive these rewards. Conversely, *if* you don't achieve those results, *then* you will incur these costs. Both the positive and negative consequences need to be specified in the same precise language as the expected behavior.

Achieving agreed-upon goals should always result in the praise and recognition of everyone involved in the project. This recognition has practical consequences because these successful employees gain more credibility with management and will have more of a say in future planning and decision making. They have demonstrated that they can be counted on to deliver on their commitment to implement a change. In addition, they may receive benefits such as more attractive work assignments, added managerial responsibility, and possibly substantive rewards in the case of the attainment of major goals.

It is even more important to specify the negative consequences of failing to live up to commitments. Such failures can be disastrous for the project and could negate all of the work done by others. Those who don't do what they promised will, at the very least, lose the respect and admiration of their colleagues and their boss. For some, the threat of losing face in the eyes of their associates is enough to motivate them to achieve promised goals. In most situations, it's useful to also link the loss of tangible benefits to the failure to achieve promised goals.

Much as you might be tempted to act like the Red Queen in *Alice in Wonderland* and say, "Off with their heads," there are more effective ways to promulgate negative consequences. In team meetings and publications, failures can be publicly acknowledged as a form of social censure and incentive. Rather than saying, "You screwed up," you can clearly and concisely state the facts. "You guys didn't achieve the results you promised you would." People who don't live up to commitments may lose their position of influence within the group and will probably get less attractive assignments until they do. Their failure should be clearly recorded for consideration at annual review time, meaning their salary, bonus, and advancement opportunities will be affected.

While there's no need for public humiliation, others need to know there have been negative consequences. When sending such a message, it is useful to include an optimistic message about the future. "Because the X team was not able to produce all that it had committed to, its members have not been invited to this celebration. In my discussion with them, we reviewed concrete steps they can take to make sure this never happens again. They're good people who feel badly about not meeting their goals, and I know they won't let it happen again. They know I have confidence in their capacity to be an important part of our continuing efforts. If you see any of them in the next few days, you might let them know you're available to help them if they should need it in the future. Now let's celebrate all that you have accomplished."

Each work situation provides rewards that can be denied to non-performers and punishments that can be enforced. When it comes to deciding upon the magnitude of the negative consequences, you can follow Gilbert and Sullivan's advice and "Let the punishment suit the crime."

If you spell out the negative consequences of nonperformance at the beginning, it's easier, and far less frightening, to enforce them at the end. After all, "we both agreed to this before we began this implementation." Prior to the launch, you can usually get workers to agree to enforce the agreement. "We both understand the importance of achieving these first-phase goals in the implementation. And I'm very confident that you will succeed. Therefore, there is every reason to expect that you and your team will receive the financial bonus due those who fully contribute to the project's success. Neither one of us wants your team to miss out on the bonus because they didn't deliver on their commitment."

If you're unsure what to impose as a negative consequence, ask the other person. "Given that you think your team can achieve these first-phase goals, what would be a reasonable negative consequence for any team that fails to get these results?" Often they'll suggest something more severe than you would have thought of imposing—especially if they think they're determining how those "other" likely nonperformers will be treated.

Managers who might be hesitant to actually follow through and punish someone now have the employees' prior agreement to use in holding them accountable. Because the agreement has been made in public, the manager also knows that if he fails to enforce the agreement, he'll lose the respect of all the other parties.

While the workers are implementing the change, leaders at all levels have duties and responsibilities they must agree to perform. These include providing assistance and coaching, monitoring progress, reassigning resources, and possibly changing the implementation plan.

As leader you must also spell out the negative consequences that you will be subject to if you fail to live up to your commitments. Sometimes these can be humorous, and slightly humiliating, as well as corrective: agreeing to dress in an outrageous outfit, sitting on the plank in the water tank while employees throw balls to dunk you, working for a full day on the line or in the field. Whatever the penalty, the leader must hold both himself and the other senior managers accountable for doing exactly what they promised.

Link Performance to Larger Goals

Spending all this time on the details means employees can sometimes lose sight of the bigger picture. Just as the proverbial stonemasons may forget they're building a cathedral, someone writing software code may not be thinking about how the customers will use the product. In a similar way, work teams may lose track of how their cost cutting can impact the overall profitability, which could mean the plant will stay open and they'll have a job. After spelling out the little "ifs" and "thens," it's useful to remind employees of the linkage between their specific tasks and the larger change initiative.

Linking the work of particular people to high-level goals is fun because you are helping people understand the larger significance of what they're doing. That's bound to make them feel good. When something is going to bring all this joy, leaders are often tempted to be the exclusive storyteller. But this is a good situation in which to employ the "ask, don't tell" technique.

Ask one of the participants how she thinks the actions of the group will contribute to larger organizational objectives. "Wendy, what connections do you see between what we're doing here and the company's overall commitment to improved customer service?" Wendy will probably have a good answer but if she doesn't, be prepared with another question. "How will what we're doing make it easier for people to do business with us?" If not Wendy, someone else will have an answer, and soon others will begin describing links to the larger picture.

If they don't do it spontaneously, make sure they see the connection between the big picture and their personal situation by asking, "Can anyone see a way increased customer satisfaction might improve your work situation?" As they make the links, you can sit back and relish the commitment and wisdom of your team.

Plan for Problems

No, the recommendation isn't to plan to create problems but rather to plan how to deal with any that might arise. Identifying potential problems and preparing coping tactics serves many purposes. Stop and think. What typically bad things can happen when people don't have a plan for addressing a sudden crisis?

Employees could later claim that because they didn't know what to do, they thought it best to do no harm, so they did nothing. They use the lack of a plan as an excuse for why they failed to live up to their commitment and as a justification for why they shouldn't be held accountable. Discussing an emergency plan in advance eliminates this escape from accountability.

If you ask for ideas about how to handle different problems that could come up, you'll probably hear innovative solutions that hadn't occurred to you. Here's another place in which you can use ask, don't tell. Posing these questions doesn't require fancy language, but you should be alert to some possible problems in asking. Imagine a manager talking to one of his direct reports.

"Jud, I'm really glad we understand exactly what each of us needs to do to implement this new system. And I feel confident that we'll be able to do it. If everything goes well we should be able to beat the deadlines, but let's think about what might go wrong along the way. What problems can you imagine happening?"

When Jud starts describing potential problems, encourage him to keep identifying as many problems as possible before he, or you, start to suggest solutions. Otherwise, he'll get so involved with solving one or two problems that he won't even think of the many other things that could go wrong. As he mentions potential problems, acknowledge his ideas and encourage him further. "Good thinking. I hadn't thought about that as a problem. Those are good insights. What else might conceivably go wrong?"

When you ask employees to think of things that might block the implementation, be prepared for them to draw a blank. "I don't know, boss. I can't think of any problems. You've done such a good job of laying this out in detail, we should have smooth sailing. We've never done this before, but I like it and hope we'll make it a standard part of our planning."

Coming up with this kind of adulation, sincere or not, suggests that Jud is pretty savvy. He may be using flattery as a way to avoid answering your question. You can use the same tactic for dealing with the "I don't know" answer as was described in Chapter 6. Acknowledge that he may not have any idea at this moment, then restate the question. "Glad you like the plan, Jud. I agree it should be successful. Problems are a part of everything we do, even with great planning, and I'd really like to hear your ideas about any possible problems, large or small, we might encounter."

By agreeing with what he said, you acknowledge that you heard him, and by repeating the question, you let him know you expect him to answer. This will probably start speculation about possible barriers but, if not, there are a number of simple additional questions you can ask.

"Look, you've had a lot of experience with projects like this. Based on your experiences, what kinds of things have you seen happen in other situations?" Or "Just let your imagination run wild." The wording isn't as critical as letting Jud know that you want to hear his thoughts and that you aren't going to bail him out by answering for him.

If you sense he really can't think of any problems, then lead him through the various points in the plan where you can foresee a problem and ask what challenges he thinks might arise at each crucial point in the plan. When you get down to these kinds of specifics, employees who have been having trouble answering will begin to give you answers. Those who have only been playing dumb will now have little excuse for not telling you their ideas. If they still fail to list any dangers, then this becomes a time when you can teach them how to analyze the difficulties inherent in the plan.

After employees have done a good job listing problems, you can then begin inquiring about their ideas on how to deal with each one. Encourage them to go into detail and be ready to give them personalized praise when they suggest innovative solutions. "That's great, Jud. I never would have thought of it. That would save us money and solve the problem immediately."

If they say, "I don't know how to handle that. I've never encountered it before, and I wouldn't know where to begin," what can you say? If it's plausible that they would not know how to deal with a problem or would lack the necessary authority to handle it, then tell them what they should do. If you think they do know but don't want to tell you what they're thinking, then you can probe some more. "Let's think about this. If you were stuck for a solution on how to deal with this situation, what could you do?"

"Call you" might be their first suggestion. Ultimately, you may want them to call you, but for most things you probably want them to assume responsibility before dumping it on you. Even so, you can still acknowledge the possible validity of their answer. "Yes, in some situations you could call me, but let's say you couldn't get in touch with me. What would you do?"

They may still claim ignorance as a way to get you to give them the answer. With concern, and not condescension, you can inquire again. "If I was completely unavailable, and your life depended on it, where would you turn to find a solution? Who else could you ask?" These kinds of questions invariably produce answers. In fact, often employees are surprised at how resourceful they can be when they put their mind to it.

In most cases, employees who can't think of many problems or solutions have suddenly gone dumb for a reason. They know what you're doing. They understand that by your asking these questions and getting them to answer, you are taking away some of the excuses they could have used to stop moving forward on the implementation.

By getting workers to identify problems and generate possible solutions, you help them prepare for almost all eventualities. The vast majority of employees like being prepared and they'll be more confident they can fulfill their commitment. Most important, you'll have eliminated potential roadblocks to the progress of the project.

It's tempting to adopt a zero-tolerance policy toward excuses. This absolutistic approach has a bravura sound and plays well in movies, but in real life it's less plausible. In reality, extreme extenuating circumstances will arise for which no one could plan and exceptions will need to be made. Work with the group to itemize such threats and develop a plan for how to cope with the challenge. "Clearly, if we have to double production to meet excessive demands at the end of the quarter, we'll have to temporarily shelve the special weekly meetings on root-cause analyses. Once the new quarter begins, we'll have to double the time we spend doing our root-cause analyses in order to make up for the weeks we skipped."

While granting room for acts of God and other truly exceptional conditions, it is sometimes useful to list extenuating circumstances that will *not* be accepted. Taking the time to do so is worthwhile when dealing with individuals and groups that have a history of failing to live up to their commitments. You've probably heard the excuses so often that you could provide the list for them. Don't. Keep probing to get them to acknowledge some of the "impossible roadblocks" they've encountered in the past. Then get everyone to agree they won't let things like those on the list stymie progress.

Decide How to Communicate Progress

On complex tasks with multiple groups, it's especially important to regularly communicate how things are progressing. You can begin this discussion by getting people to itemize times and situations in which other team members will most need communication. Then you can talk about when people might forget to communicate (e.g., when problems arise or when we're overworked).

After laying this practical background for the importance of communication, you can then get down to specifics. Discuss how frequently people will communicate, the content of the messages, in what form they'll communicate (such as e-mails, faxes, conference calls) and deadlines by when the messages will be sent.

No hard-and-fast rules exist for how and when people should communicate. In critical situations, daily and even hourly communication of results may be called for; in other situations, weekly or perhaps monthly progress reports may suffice. Often much more communication is needed at the beginning of an implementation than in Stages 4 and 5. You and the group can make these assessments.

The one absolute is that people must communicate about problems as soon as they arise. In addition to describing the problem, employees should tell what solutions they are pursuing and possibly ask for help from the group. The goal is to alert others so they can coordinate their activities with the latest developments. This can also be a time to seek assistance from others to help a struggling individual, or group, meet its time deadline.

Sometimes people issue advanced warning about not being able to deliver on a promise as a way to protect themselves in case they fail. You'll want to let people know that such posturing is unacceptable, and you need to alert them the moment you sense they may be doing so. "Look, Jud, I'm probably being too sensitive here, but it sounds as though you might be covering yourself in case you don't meet your deadline. I hope not. Am I misperceiving this?" If Jud wasn't trying to pre-position an excuse, he'll nondefensively deny it. "I can see how you might think that, but, no, I was just wondering out loud." If he was doing some preemptory positioning, he'll probably get self-righteous and deny any such posturing. You can then go along with his protests because you know he got the message that he won't be able to use this excuse with you.

People want to hear back from you after they've communicated their progress to you. Providing feedback is easy in a conversation, but if you receive something in writing—from a note to a multipage report—it's a good idea to respond in writing. Your message can be as simple as saying you received the report and you're pleased with what has been accomplished. Or you might want to comment on a few specifics. Doing so is an easy way to introduce some encouraging personalized praise. Obviously, if you see potential problems, you'll identify each and ask what their plan is for dealing with them if they arise.

Publicly Commit to Accountability

Fortunately, when most employees give you their word that they'll achieve the benchmarks of the implementation by the time deadline, you can believe them. With people like that, there's little need for an explicit public agreement to complete the assigned goals.

Then there are the other people. After you've been burned by individuals or groups who haven't lived up to their promises, you learn it may sometimes be necessary to spell out a clear, unambiguous statement of agreement. It may seem childish, but with the worst offenders you may even need to have them sign their name or to explicitly give verbal agreement. "Okay, you're committing to getting it done. Agreed?"

What could happen if you settle for a head nod or a wink instead of outright words of agreement? What if they fail to deliver and you say, "But you said you would get your portion completed by today." Like a child, they will respond, "I didn't say that." Technically, of course, they're correct. Such dissembling suggests the person has a much deeper problem with honesty that needs to be addressed separately.

MAKING ACCOUNTABILITY A PART OF THE CULTURE

After the accountability discussion and agreement, it is time to make it happen. Spelling out the action plan and benchmarks in specifics makes it easy for the groups and the leader to monitor progress. When employees fall behind (they're probably aware that they're not meeting objectives), a gentle nudge can be used before issuing dire warnings or making threats.

When employees fulfill their end of the bargain, it's your chance to give them the rewards they've earned. It's always enjoyable to shower subordinates with praise and rewards. Making a public show of this recognition not only honors the recipients but also shows everyone that you live up to your promises.

Up to this point we've focused on using recognition, praise, and minor tangible rewards as incentives to motivate people to implement change.

To institutionalize the change as the new way of doing things, formal rewards—such as salary, bonuses, and special incentives—must also be linked to continuous performance of the new behavior pattern.

If they're not aligned, the language of change can become window dressing. We probably all know of sales organizations that declare "The customer is our No. 1 priority" and then base decisions solely on gross sales and largely ignore customer satisfaction ratings. Or take the many research universities that proclaim their overarching goal of delivering superb undergraduate education. Beginning professors soon learn their time is better spent writing articles for publication than in preparing lectures or working one-on-one with undergraduate students.

Realigning the formal performance plan is senior management's responsibility. Realignment means adjusting the formal structure so that it reinforces only people who adopt the new approach and stop using the old one. Such changes in the system of salary increases, bonuses, and promotions are sure to produce resistance by those who benefit from the current system. Leaders must be prepared to expend the time and energy that it'll take to deal with the conflicts. Unless the formal reward system provides incentives for the *new* set of behaviors, no amount of activation, communication, or catchy slogans will be enough to sustain the change.

We often hear it said that people are in their "comfort zone" when doing things in the same old way. It might be more accurate to describe them as being in their "profit zone." Employees know how to succeed in the old system and know how to make it work to their benefit. Realigning the reward structure will negatively impact their self-interest and that's what makes them uncomfortable.

Plans for this realignment of rewards should be developed from the very beginning and should be announced as part of the launch of the initiative. At the core of the realignment is the annual performance review. It is critical that behaviors consistent with the new approach are measured in this review and that financial rewards are directly linked to excellence on those measures.

Just like Peg did with her pet peeve, you can let employees know what you will and won't accept. You can let them know the consequences of success and failure. And by following through on your statements, you can create a work environment in which not only are people's desks clean at night but they'll be responsible for their commitments to maintain the changes you've implemented.

Chapter

SUSTAINING ENTHUSIASM FOR CHANGE

No matter how brilliant the CEO's launch speech or how spiffy the T-shirts and coffee mugs given out at the kickoff meetings, employees will have trouble staying energized during the long process of a major implementation. A lack of success during Stage 2 will sap people's enthusiasm and make them dream of the pleasures of the old way of doing things. To maintain their motivation, they need a continuing source of energy—*you*.

Building and maintaining motivation is a key responsibility of those leading the implementation. Some managers feel uncomfortable with the idea that they must be motivators. As with so many high-altitude labels, this one doesn't accurately capture the actual task. Leaders don't necessarily need to be charismatic or inspirational, but they must master some of the nuts and bolts of how to keep people moving forward. Here are some ideas and actions you can use to sustain people's enthusiasm for change.

THE REFLECTION PRINCIPLE

After a Chinese dinner we often crack open a fortune cookie, expecting to read about the good things in our future—perhaps wealth, travel, or romance. Once my rosy anticipation was rudely disrupted by a fortune that posed a question: "Are you a sun or a moon?" At first I was surprised, yet the more I considered the question the more engaging it became. The sun and moon metaphor is open to many interpretations. I thought it was asking, "Are you a source of energy or are you an inert body?"

To lead an implementation, you must be a sun. Your team's degree of enthusiasm will reflect your energy. If your behavior suggests eager anticipation, a readiness for challenges, and a celebratory reaction to the successes of others, then you'll be surrounded by a team that's similarly motivated. In contrast, if you walk around worried and uncertain or with a sense of being overburdened, those are the emotions you'll see in the faces of your teammates.

All changes have their good days and bad, their successes and failures. Focus on the negatives, and you'll be negative and so will your employees. Emphasize the positives, and your demeanor will encourage others to do the same. This doesn't mean you always have to be a Pollyanna. It does mean you can't be a Scrooge. If you'll express confidence in the goal and in your team, you'll soon ignite their passion. And passion *is* required to make major changes successful and lasting.

SOURCES OF ENERGY

Big change initiatives usually go on for many months and sometimes years. Leaders must be devoted to the change and its complete implementation. Believing in what they are doing and what the change is going to do for the organization inspires and sustains most leaders. When leaders don't feel that kind of total devotion, the frustrations of Stage 2 and employees' resistance wear on them and they soon give up.

Knowing that a successful change will advance your career and the well-being of the organization can be one source of motivation. There's nothing like some personal benefit to inspire you to do all the repetitive daily work of execution.

Renewing your energy is sometimes a matter of stepping back from the process for a day and reconnecting with the ultimate benefits of the project for your organization. One of the functions of group update meetings and annual retreats is to recharge people's internal power sources. Experiencing the excitement of the senior executives in a company can also reignite the energy of the change champions out in the field.

No matter how much you love your organization, the change initiative, or your own career prospects, these things won't provide enough oomph to keep you energized all the time. You'll need other sources of energy. Let's look at some.

Focusing on People

A renewable source of energy is needed to keep you and your whole team going throughout the implementation—and it's the people. This source of power comes from being involved with the details of how the change is playing out in the lives of the individuals on the team.

Change happens down at the level of the individual who does the step-by-step work of making the new plan a reality. By helping each team member, whether a middle manager or a frontline worker, attain their work objectives and their personal development goals, you'll have many things to celebrate. Acknowledging their achievements along the way enables you to front-load rewards to keep each of them engaged.

Setting Personal Goals

To get to the great reservoir of untapped motivation inside employees, managers must work with each of their direct reports to help them set their own personal achievement goals. These personal goals can either relate directly to the change itself or relate to personal growth.

When it comes to the change initiative, each person might set dates for how quickly he or she will learn the new software or how quickly she'll begin using it in her daily work. In the customer-service arena, milestones might be set for improvements in their personal customer service ratings. Or goals could be set for the number of actions taken consistently with the new initiative (e.g., the number of phone calls a car salesperson makes within one month of a purchase to make sure each new owner is satisfied).

In addition to setting personal goals directly linked to the change initiative, you should also encourage individuals to set personal advancement goals. The idea here is that working on the change initiative can provide an ideal forum in which to work on personal development.

One employee might want to improve her skills in financial analysis as a way to help herself grow and to better contribute to the change initiative. Each class she successfully completes could count as an achievement to be celebrated. Another individual's focus could be on improving his communication skills. He might have subgoals linked to the number of presentations he makes to the group. Giving a speech might be second nature to you, but for someone frightened of public speaking, giving even a 30-second report to the group could be a major accomplishment.

Because most people don't spontaneously think of linking their personal goals to an organizational change, they'll benefit from some coaching by you. These individualized development goals can often come directly out of the employee's most recent annual performance review. Employees will work harder because you've helped them link the organizational change to their own self-interest. By getting them to set progressive personal goals, you'll have more opportunities to motivate them by encouraging and then celebrating their successes along the way.

In truth, the only way employees can sustain their motivation on a challenging implementation is to experience personal benefit while helping move the organization forward. You can tap this private source of energy by focusing on each individual's personal growth goals.

Formal education programs have great value, but nothing compares to the direct in situ coaching of a manager. Managers can help their people achieve their personal growth goals during the ups and downs of everyday work life. When they do, they show respect and loyalty for the members of their team. You can be that kind of manager during a change implementation.

Setting Team Outcome Goals

Every implementation plan should have quantifiable milestone goals as well as an ultimate goal. By establishing subgoals at various points—such as the 25 percent, 50 percent, and 75 percent levels of completion—you create opportunities to praise groups of employees for their hard work and to inspire them to keep moving forward. These goals can involve two kinds of outcomes: number of projects completed or actual results.

The early stages of implementation build the foundation for later success, so progress is often measured in terms of projects completed rather than positive business results. For example, successfully installing parts of the new software system can be celebrated as a completed project. Designing a training program to teach the new system may be another project, and actually getting groups to complete these educational programs could be a follow-up step. Such foundational projects, even though they aren't yet producing tangible results, deserve to be celebrated.

Once the groundwork has been completed, production outcomes can be measured. In a factory, for example, setting a results goal might involve progressive increases in the number of units shipped, or decreases in the scrap rate, or marginal decreases in the costs of production. For a marketing operation, the results sought might be number of responses and/or sales following each new promotion. In improving customer satisfaction, milestones could include increases in scores on a customer survey or perhaps a percentage reduction in the number of complaints.

Setting Team Process Goals

Just as individuals can set personal goals during an implementation, a work group can set goals for *how* it wants to function as a team. Completing the change will most likely require a great deal of teamwork. So it would be useful for the team to decide upon some goals for how they want to deal with one another.

Guided by the leader, the team needs to talk about topics such as communication practices, decision-making processes, conflict resolution, sharing work responsibilities, and supporting one another. It's tough to put quantitative benchmarks on these kinds of more qualitative processes. Just talking about them gets employees thinking about how they are dealing with one another and gives them an incentive to behave at their best.

Getting the team to discuss specific ways to make these improvements lets the team members know the leader will be monitoring these processes. Because the goals relating to the group process are usually subjective, leaders have the added responsibility to observe and provide feedback to the team.

This subjective nature provides leaders with the freedom to generously front-load praise on even the smallest examples of good teamwork that occur in the early stages of change. A lone case of someone sharing information retrieved from a database or a single instance of a team member thanking another could be worthy of acknowledgment in a team meeting. "Cheri, I really appreciated the way you distributed those contact lists you developed from your research on the database. That's teamwork at the most fundamental level. Let's all keep it up." Similarly, "Roberto, I was impressed with the way you thanked Shana for her assistance. We all need praise and acknowledgment for our contributions. Way to go."

By publicly recognizing these process achievements, you also give people the sense that this kind of team behavior is increasingly common. If a particular person isn't acting like a good team member, he'll feel that he should begin to, because he thinks everyone else is doing it. Shaping employees' definition of the social reality of their work environment is another inducement for them to live that new reality.

Celebrating Little Victories

If you go through life waiting to celebrate the big victories, you probably won't spend much money on party favors and catering. Very few of us will win an Oscar, score the game-winning touchdown, or grace the cover of a national magazine. What we will accomplish are the small significant milestones in the daily routine of our work. Those little victories are well worth recognizing because they provide another opportunity to build enthusiasm and to neutralize employees' fears about change.

Many leaders are so committed to reaching the top of the mountain as quickly as possible that they overlook the importance of reaching small plateaus. In Stages 2 and 3, forget the question of whether the glass is half full or half empty. Just getting enough water to cover the bottom of the glass is a major accomplishment.

Instead of celebrating these small, early victories, many leaders do the exact opposite. They focus only on the next big goals that must be achieved. Rather than using the first half of a team meeting to laud workers for their efforts to date, they discuss how much more has yet to be accomplished. Planning for the next push is important, but it's better to do it after you've recognized how much the team has already done. Knowing management values their efforts will motivate employees to take on the challenges ahead.

The little victories must be linked to real and significant accomplishments. This is not an exercise designed to boost everyone's self-esteem by offering a plaque for merely showing up at work. The size of the celebration is linked to the magnitude of the accomplishment. Small goals may only deserve a one-minute pause during a meeting to announce the result and recognize those who did it. Major milestones warrant more time, resources, and rewards.

As a final reason for honoring little victories, think back to some of the major events you've attended to recognize achieving the Stage 5 completion of a major change. The celebration usually takes place long after the goal was actually accomplished. As a result it feels anticlimactic for many of the employees involved. They reached the peak weeks or months ago and for them the really significant events were conquering the challenges that arose on the way to the top. Those en route victories are the essence of life and of successful changes. Leaders need to celebrate them along the way.

Publicizing Progress

If you overlook opportunities to celebrate little victories, you also miss an important forum in which you can give everyone a sense of how well the change is progressing. In large organizations, work teams are often geographically separated and unaware of what other groups are doing. Employees develop what is called "pluralistic ignorance." That's when we're all unaware of what other people are doing, so we infer they are doing about the same as us.

Just as early philosophers put the earth at the center of the universe, employees tend to define reality in terms of what they or their immediate work groups are doing. As long as the group is advancing nicely, that self-centered conception of the progress of the change is fine.

Employees who haven't experienced much success, or who haven't even started the implementation, conclude the change is a failure. Based on their pessimistic view, they decide they no longer need to support the change.

Communicating progress is especially important during major change initiatives in large organizations. It is quite common for only one or two groups to have great early success with the new approach. Since most people are not making progress, they assume no one is. The leader has to highlight these few early successes and use them as a way to encourage the groups that are not yet making headway.

You can help employees get an accurate picture of the overall progress of the change initiative by keeping them informed of recent successes of other teams. Because you are aware of certain successes, it's easy to falsely assume everyone has heard about it. They probably haven't and, even if they have, it's worth repeating and hearing more than once or twice. As you tell the story you can help people see the implications this success has for their work and for the larger goals of the change initiative.

During implementation, the leader takes on the role of town crier, personally sharing the good news with everyone she encounters. Repeating success stories creates motivation by giving employees a sense of widespread progress, and it provides an incentive for others to get on the bandwagon. Newsletters, bulletins, and formal speeches are also useful, and nothing beats word of mouth to convey a compelling sense of progress.

A large-scale example of the failure to publicize progress came from a Fortune 500 corporation that had an organization-wide cultural change initiative to foster innovation. As part of the initiative, business units around the world sent in their best examples of innovative projects they planned to implement. The teams that submitted the 50 best proposals for innovation were honored at a major event at corporate headquarters.

Two years later during a meeting for high-potential middle managers, several attendees began lamenting the failure of the innovations award program. The basic criticism was, "Yeah, that shindig was full of fanfare about the winning proposals, but then how many of them were actually implemented? None. That's what's wrong with this company. They never..." Fortunately, a manager from corporate communications immediately spoke up. "What do you mean none of them were implemented? I personally know of forty-seven that are well into execution." It's the job of the person at the top, who is leading the initiative, to communicate success and it's the responsibility of managers down in the middle of the organization to retell those tales. Communicating success stories is especially important in Stages 2 and 3 when there isn't a great deal of progress. Too often we wait for the really big achievements of Stages 4 and 5 to tout successes. Start publicizing successes early and often.

REACTIONS TO SETBACKS

No matter how well you plan the implementation, problems will always pop up. At the beginning you expect them and are mentally prepared to take them on. But when the change is coming out of Stage 3 and into Stage 4, you're expecting a rapid ascent. Suddenly, a major problem develops. It could be that a key machine breaks down or a piece of software crashes. Perhaps a major customer becomes unhappy and cancels a big order.

Setbacks that occur after we thought we'd turned the corner on the change can devastate your motivation. A continuing string of failures at the beginning can play havoc with a leader's enthusiasm. The reflection principle kicks in after failures as well as after successes. If the leader expresses disappointment and sagging confidence, the whole team will soon join the vent-a-thon. Even team members who are ready to deal with the new problem will start to shut down. The vultures begin to circle when people give off an aura that the change initiative is not going to be long for this world.

While planning the implementation, you should also plan how to deal with major setbacks. You may not be able to predict exactly where and when the problems will arise, but you know they will happen. Even lacking specifics, you can develop a general strategy for how you will react to anything unexpected.

How should you react to major setbacks? Emotionally, you can't help but be frustrated and possibly angry. It's only natural to express some of these negative emotions when your progress is blocked. Keep it brief and do it in private. When you're with the team in public, whether on the work site or in a bar at the end of the day, allow yourself only a single groan of frustration or a few choice words. Within a matter of seconds, you have to come back more determined than ever.

It is vitally important that your public lament not include any criticism of higher-level managers who are leading the change. If you think some top-level managers were responsible for the problem, tell them in private. Don't share your feelings with your whole team. Remember the reflection principle: the energy you radiate is what will come back at you. Even in cases where clearly someone else in the organization is at fault, it's better to just politely acknowledge that others make decisions we don't always understand, but that's just the nature of large organizations. Get people focused on the key question of what do we do now to make this change a success.

In the same way that you acknowledge employees' negative emotions as part of the activation process, you should let people briefly express their negative emotional reactions to the setback. No hard-and-fast rules exist about how many minutes to allow for this grieving. As a guide, watch for any sign that the venting of emotions is turning into a discussion of why the change is a mistake and will never work. That is the moment to assert yourself and speak forcefully about the constructive things that now need to be done.

When it comes to remedial action, you may want to think of your group as a sports team that had just made it into the semifinals. Trite as the refrain may be, there's some truth in the sportscaster's oft-repeated wisdom that this is when true champions ramp their game up to the next level. Just as sports teams are capable of a higher degree of performance and motivation, so too are work teams.

Simplistic as it may sound, even the hardest-working individuals are capable of higher performance during an emergency. They may not be able to sustain this new level for weeks; however, they can function there long enough to deal with the emergency and get the change back on track.

In addition to making your own personal plans for how you'll react to setbacks, you can get the team to do the same thing. You may meet some initial resistance along the lines of "Why should we be negative? It's as though we expect trouble." If you persist and get employees to list potential problems and possible solutions, you'll be amazed at how quickly everyone joins in. This is similar to the planning for problems that was discussed in Chapter 9 as part of establishing accountability.

ALTERNATIVE SOURCES OF ENERGY

Completing a major change is a great deal of work, demanding large amounts of physical and psychological energy. The initial source of your energy comes from the anticipation of the rewards for successfully completing the change. That energy can be quickly expended when you get caught up in the demands of implementation in Stages 2 and 3.

Because successes may be few during the initial stages, you will need alternative sources of energy to sustain you. If you really identify with the individuals on your team, their success in achieving their personal and team goals can provide an important added boost. The key is that you honestly care about helping your employees develop and grow. When you do, you'll naturally feel invigorated by their personal achievements.

Even with such vicarious pleasures, a morning will come when you aren't sure you have the energy to again take on all the challenges of another day. Knowing the effects of the reflection principle, you can't let your lack of motivation infect the group. What can you do? Fake it.

If you do a really good job of pretending as though you're excited and confident, an amazing thing usually happens. While you are acting fully engaged, you'll encounter someone who is genuinely excited about one of her personal accomplishments. Because you sincerely care about your employees, the reflection principle will operate in reverse: the employee's enthusiasm will spark your reserves and soon you'll be glowing too.

Not all of your motivation can come from inside the organization. The excitement about the project itself and team members' accomplishments has to be supplemented with alternative sources of energy. What truly renews your spirit? If you don't have a ready answer to that question, please give it some thought.

All of us have people, activities, and places that feed our souls. Often it comes from time spent with family members, old friends, and loved ones. Or it could be associated with exercise, travel, shopping, spiritual practice, or plain old sleep. Most of us can think of a particular place—ocean, mountains, waterfalls, or meadows—that enables us to get centered and reenergized.

Take a few minutes right now to make a list of what reinvigorates you. Yes, actually write it down because the miracle of activation comes from doing, not just from thinking. Now look at your monthly schedule. How much time have you been setting aside for these uplifting activities? Next, plan when and how you can allocate a few sacred hours each week to renew yourself. Find something you can do in the next week to restore your energy. Don't kid yourself into thinking you can wait for the holiday break that's coming next month. Do something soon—now.

While work teams seldom have these natural sources of energy, ways exist to recharge a group's juices as well. Anything that breaks the monotony and introduces an element of play and fun can be useful.

Surprise visits by performers, magicians, and other forms of entertainment can rouse many employees' sagging spirits on a slow Wednesday afternoon. Juvenile as it sounds, inviting a clown to make balloon animals, for instance, will provide everyone with a chuckle and a souvenir to take home to their children or grandchildren.

Perhaps you could don a ridiculous outfit to brighten people's mood. The sillier the activity the better it seems to distract and enliven the whole team. Don't be put off by the few dour-faced Resisters who will use these activities to condemn you and the change. Instead, notice how many people will energetically talk about these events for weeks afterward. If you can't think of any fun surprises, ask a few people on your team for suggestions. You'll have some people who are more than happy to perform or pull some outrageous stunt.

CONTINUOUS CHANGE

Many management experts and charismatic CEOs during the dot-com era gave the impression that change should be a part of everyone's daily diet. Continuous change was put forward as the ideal for organizations and individuals. Ideally, continuous change sounds good, but the reality is startlingly different. By necessity, a great deal of continuity and stability must exist in an organization to balance the change.

The organizations that seem to be changing all the time do it in a selective way. Seldom is it the same business unit that is taking the lead on each new change. One unit may drive a particular change initiative. Then it slows down to stabilize this new way of doing business. Meanwhile, a different unit in another part of the organization is initiating a different change that will go through its J Curve and similarly reach a new plateau. When looked at from a distance, it may appear that the organization is continuously changing, but that doesn't mean every unit is simultaneously moving forward at the same pace.

The plateau that occurs after Stage 5 is a necessary part of the process. New policies and procedures must be refined to produce maximum results. Departmental boundaries, responsibilities, and leadership assignments need to be realigned to take advantage of new opportunities and efficiencies. Although such activities may seem small by comparison to the overall change, they too require individuals to make adjustments in their daily work lives.

Use the reduced demands during the plateau following a major change to give employees an opportunity to take care of other responsibilities that have been neglected during the heavy-lifting phases. This period also provides a chance for workers to slow down and renew themselves. This renewal not only restores people's energy but it also gives them time to experiment with new ideas that frequently become the basis of the next big change.

As a change leader, you are enticing people to enter the small world that you've created. Your generic change speech paints a picture of the beauty at the top of the mountain. Your enthusiasm gives them a sense that they can also reach those new heights. Your knowledge gives them confidence that they have an expert who can guide them to the top. Your sensitivity to their feelings, the risks they're taking, and the burdens they're assuming helps make them comfortable taking on this heavier load. Because you allowed them to participate in defining the route to the top, they feel it's their trip as well as yours.

Before you begin the change, take time to think about the small world that you want to create for your people as they go through the change. Simplify your message and put it into terms that are meaningful and memorable to everyone. Work to identify the essence of what the change means to the organization, your customers, and your people. That is your song. By repeatedly singing it and using activation techniques to help employees change, you'll lead them to a whole new world.

Chapter

CREATING A CULTURE OF CHANGE

Implementing one or more specific changes is fine. But what if you, like most leaders, yearn to create a culture of change? How can you so weave innovation into the daily routine that it becomes a widely shared value? That's a worthy but daunting goal. Where do you start on something that big?

My suggestion is to take a clue from Disneyland. At the so-called happiest place on earth, social engineering is a fine art. Take, for example, the ride known as "It's a Small World." For the uninitiated, this involves riding in a small boat through a fake cavern depicting foreign cultures while being assaulted by that insidious song: "It's a small world...after all...it's a small world after all."

Though dreaded by many adults, the ride is brilliant at creating an environment that's utterly transforming. It takes diverse (often recalcitrant) individuals and turns them into a unified group that is literally singing the same song. The ride's designers not only know how to produce mass change but they do it by the boatload every few minutes and then repeat it over and over again.

What lessons can we learn from this? Which of its techniques can we use to create a new cultural value in an organization? The central principle is repetition. You hear that song over and over. It never stops. Even when the sound track pauses, you often hear a bit of the refrain in another language. So not only is the message repeatedly beamed at you but it's also tailored to people from other cultures.

Another lesson involves the song's content and style. It captures the complex message of global unity and shared humanity in a simple phrase. Plus, the melody and voices are positive and upbeat.

Further, the ride is set up so that enthusiasm builds as each rider reacts to new stimuli. While you're marveling at the Eskimos and the walrus displays, your companion is joyfully reacting to the upcoming Hawaiian dancers. His or her enthusiasm increases yours.

Notice, too, that the experience takes place inside a giant box. That ensures that you're cut off from all external distractions. Your attention is focused on what's illuminated in your immediate line of sight. So what we have is a simple positive message that is repeated over and over and an environment that surrounds people with the message while multiplying the emotions of others to heighten the experience.

Let's see how you could use those principles to begin creating a culture of change at work. The example that follows will focus on the concept of innovation. But you can use the same approach with other cultural values you might want to create, such as customer service, entrepreneurship, or replacing a command-and-control culture with one that's employee-oriented.

SURROUNDING PEOPLE WITH INFORMATION

To instill your value—innovation in this case—repetition is a key. Metaphorically, it's your "song" that you'll be singing over and over. The first step is to distill the message to a word or sentence. At the beginning that may be something as straightforward as "innovation" or "continual change." Or to instill an emphasis on service, you may start with something as conventional as "The customer is No. 1." Eventually you'll hit upon a catchphrase or symbol that captures the message for your employees and organization. Most often these phrases emerge from the ranks during the process of implementation.

Once you've distilled your message, you can begin to think about how you can surround people with that message. Although banners, posters, bulletin boards, and other visual representations may not be enough in themselves to get people to change, they transmit an important underlying message. The core idea you're seeking to convey is that you want employees to innovate.

You'll be creative in devising ways that you can repeat your message, but here are some ideas to get you started:

• *Begin every team meeting with a discussion of innovation.* This can be a quick summary of an important change an individual or team is initiating or an update on an existing implementation. If you have more time, individuals can report on changes they are currently implementing. I once observed this at work in a firm that was promoting the value of safety. Every meeting began with a one-minute identification of escape routes in case of fire and a designation of a meeting point in case of evacuation. The consistency of the message emphasized its continuing relevance.

• *Bring articles from newspapers, magazines, and journals to share.* If you're emphasizing continual change and innovation, what kind of articles are you going to bring? Clearly, you want stories about how other organizations are successfully innovating. These articles don't even need to deal with innovations in your particular industry or geographic area. As we'll see later, the stories are often more effective when they discuss innovations that differ from your own.

You can circulate a copy of an article before a meeting, and then use the opening few minutes to ask everyone to discuss what practical lesson they took away from the reading and how they are going to apply it in their work. Initially you may be the primary source of this kind of information, but you want to encourage members of the team to bring in articles and information that they have discovered too.

• *Arrange special events when the message is getting stale.* You may want to try to reengage employees' commitment by holding an educational program on innovation. Or have an outside speaker from a different department or organization talk about his or her own recent innovations to spark interest. Sending one or two of your people to visit another operation and report back on what innovative ideas they discover can also help.

• *Promote the value during informal encounters.* How can you repeat your theme when you talk to workers or send e-mails or text messages? One manager took an innovative approach. Each time he encountered coworkers, he greeted them with the question, "What's new?" In many contexts this question is rhetorical and really just another way of saying hello. But this fellow meant it literally.

When he asked workers what was new, he expected them to tell him about some innovation they were working on. He sincerely wanted to hear about something new and different they were developing. The new thing didn't have to be earthshaking, just something out of the ordinary such as an idea they were thinking about, a new procedure or new project they were starting, or a change in their work habits or manner of dealing with people.

When they told him what was new for them personally, he listened with rapt attention. He was sincerely interested in exactly what new things people were attempting. Their stories also provided an ideal time for him to express his gratitude for their innovations and to offer guidance or assistance. Almost always, he asked them to keep him informed of the outcome of the innovation. All this could transpire in a few minutes, but both the leader and the team member felt energized by the encounter. And it naturally and subtly repeated the message that the leader was committed to innovation.

If there was time, he'd tell them about someone else's innovation story he'd heard recently. He usually ended this description with a sincere question. "Is that something you think might work for you as well?" Again, this wasn't just rhetorical because he'd pause and attentively listen to their answer.

The point here isn't for you to necessarily mimic this man's approach but rather to stimulate you to think about small things you can do to surround people with information about innovation. Creating an environment that emphasizes and reemphasizes the same value may not sound exciting or significant, but when it comes to implementing a new cultural value, this is a critical part of your job.

People are watching you all the time. They notice what you talk about, what excites you, what gets your praise, and what you continually emphasize. If you want them to innovate, you have to sing that song doggedly in as many languages and ways as you can. As a leader, your job is not to come up with all the answers; instead, it's to create an environment in which others can generate innovation.

It sounds good to assert that your message should be coming at people from 360 degrees 24/7, but that's unrealistic. Regular work and goals must be completed. But while you're performing those duties, you can find small windows in which to repeat your message of innovation. Notice that in the example of including your message at every meeting, it was only a minute or two at the beginning that emphasized innovation. Similarly, you can refine your stories about innovation so that you can deliver them in less than a minute. Remember that Disney ride. The key is repetition, repetition, repetition.

PRACTICAL CREATIVITY

When you think of truly creative people, who comes to mind? Often we think of visual artists, musicians, literary figures, and Nobel Prize–winning scientists. A few years ago, Apple Computer relied on this notion with the advertising slogan "Think Different," which was coupled with oversized photos of exceptional innovators, such as Einstein and Gandhi.

What does this model of creativity mean about the rest of us? It may imply that the vast majority of us are noncreatives who can only admire the geniuses from a distance. We seem to be cast as drones who merely take the insights of others and put them into practice.

While exceptional thinkers do create truly novel ideas, much of the creativity that drives business doesn't require groundbreaking thought. Most creative business advances rely more on courage and risk-taking than exceptional thinking or a surfeit of right-brain activity.

Practical creativity often involves the transfer of an idea from one arena to another. An idea, process, or procedure that has been worked out and used in one business domain is then applied to another one. This cross-fertilization requires someone having the courage to transfer an existing solution to a field in which it has never been applied.

Take, for example, Dell Computers and Starbucks Coffee, two of the most successful corporations of the last few decades. One day as I was in line to order a sandwich at a deli, I began to marvel at the genius of Michael Dell. He came up with the idea of making a computer to the customer's specifications, much as the deli responds to the request for "a turkey on whole wheat. No mustard and light on the mayo."

This made-to-order idea isn't new. Yet for over a century, big manufacturers had instead been set on creating large inventories of a few models for the mass market. Michael Dell had the courage to think that the custom-made approach could be applied to the personal computer. This observation doesn't take away from Mr. Dell's innovation, but it illustrates the process of the transfer of existing solutions.

Another of Dell's innovations was to sell direct to customers rather than relying on retail distributors. This had been the approach of individual craftspeople from early times. What's more, Sears Roebuck had pioneered this concept on a massive scale a century or more ago with its famous catalogue. But again, Mr. Dell was willing to take the risk of applying this methodology to the distribution and sale of electronic equipment that had traditionally been sold through retail outlets.

And what about Starbucks? Small coffee stands selling espresso and cappuccinos were well-established institutions in Europe. According to the company's Web site, Howard Schultz traveled to Italy and was "impressed with the popularity of espresso bars in Milan." Schultz's genius was in having the determination to convince the founders of Starbucks that the same idea could work in Seattle.

There was even an existing name—"boutique"—that could be applied to the idea of turning the coffee shop into a store selling high-end products. Small specialty shops have a long history of catering to a niche-market segment. Shultz deserves recognition for being willing to champion such a "creative" approach to selling coffee, but let's not forget that his success was based more on daring than creative genius.

It takes exceptional bravery and guts to do something that goes against accepted wisdom. The almost universally accepted wisdom is that ideas from other industries or cultures couldn't work here. The Not Invented Here Syndrome has to be overcome to create innovation and change in established practices.

One of the most intriguing examples of this cross-fertilization is the history of the adhesive-fastening technique known as Velcro. The story is that George de Mestral of Switzerland returned from a hike, and both his clothes and his dog were covered with burrs. Generations of humans have dealt with this problem, and most of them simply stewed as they meticulously extricated the tenacious seed sacs from their clothing and pets. Instead of lamenting his fate, George de Mestral thought of transferring nature's hook-and-loop methodology to the human realm of fasteners.

The fact that virtually all practical creativity in the business world relies on the transfer of existing ideas and solutions has huge implications for how you can make innovative changes in your business. It means you'll want to do as much as possible to encourage this cross-fertilization. How?

- *Acknowledge how much wisdom your team members already possess.* Make sure workers understand you truly value their existing knowledge and that you want them to use it to generate innovation and change. Employees' personal hobbies and avocations, for example, involve technologies and practices that might be applied to your business. And experiences that employees have had in other companies and industries, or even on vacations, could have implications for your business.
- *Encourage your people to experiment in applying novel ideas, ones they already know and understand.* The simplest way to do this is through your words of encouragement. You can also do it by surrounding your employees with information. The news articles, your questions, and stories can emphasize this cross-fertilization.

A clever way to encourage the transfer of knowledge is to send one or two team members for a day to observe and learn about what works in a different industry. They might visit an organization with some obvious similarities to your own. For example, if you manage a warehouse, you could send observers to a large hospital to see how they distribute and account for their inventories of medical supplies. Or the field trip could be to very different kinds of operations, perhaps a newspaper or an auto dealership.

Sometimes just observing the practices of different areas *within* your organization can stimulate cross-fertilization. Marketing personnel could spend time with those in purchasing, for instance. In addition to promoting the transfer of solutions, these visits build relationships and respect within your company.

Many added benefits arise from sending a representative to another organization. You then can invite that outfit to send someone to spend a day in your operation. After the visit you'll want a debriefing in which you get his or her ideas about how you could improve and innovate. This can bring multiple benefits to both organizations.

Naturally, you'll want the members of your team who visited another operation to share their insights with the rest of their group. A key should be to encourage members of the team who stayed at home to think of ways they could apply the ideas their teammates bring back from the outside.

EVERYONE CAN CONTRIBUTE

Innovation is suddenly democratized once you realize that it's the transfer of existing solutions that drives business advances. That means everyone can potentially contribute.

Everyone is a broad word that's up at the 40,000-foot level, so let's bring it down to earth. Who could we include in the "everyone" category?

- *Employees who are often overlooked*. Everyone means everyone on the payroll. Think especially of those you wouldn't normally include as potential sources of creativity and innovation. Not just the usual suspects in upper management, but those at all levels of the organization. Frontline folks won't be prepared to invent a completely new business strategy for a Fortune 500 corporation, but they can suggest innovative ways to handle problems within their sphere of understanding.

- *Customers.* They can be a great source of ideas because, in a sense, they know your products and services better than anyone. Pay special attention to their complaints. Many may just want to whine about how they wish you treated them better, but a few will have concrete, doable recommendations.
- *Vendors and suppliers.* They already know something about your operations, and it's in their interest for you to be more successful. You can harvest their ideas through individual interviews or meetings in which they are included with other participants.
- *Friends, relatives, neighbors.* Virtually anyone can offer novel recommendations. Again, you could propose a trade in which you or one of your employees would visit their operations in a hunt for new solutions. It's often especially useful to get people completely outside your industry or market segment. If they're radically different, they probably don't share the same assumptions about what can and can't be done, and what will and won't work in your environment.
- *New employees*. Because much of innovation involves being willing to go against the traditionally accepted wisdom, old-timers often have on blinders that obscure new possibilities. This lesson is hard to accept because these veterans also have useful knowledge. To complicate things even more, they tend to be at the highest levels of the organization and have a vested interest in keeping things as they are.

Young people can see with clearer eyes than the lifers. Plus, many newcomers are recent graduates whose heads are full of the latest theories and research. Their ideas may not be completely realistic, but they are worth listening to.

Too often young people are regarded as liabilities rather than assets. Yet when it comes to innovative suggestions, they are one of your hidden treasures, despite their weaknesses. Yes, they've got much to learn, they're too idealistic, and they don't see the big picture. But they can provide truly different perspectives and ideas. Part of their naïveté may be a willingness to tell you what you don't want to hear in ways that long-time employees are too intimidated to mention.

• *Middle managers brought in from the outside*. These can be extremely important assets, at least for the first few months. Although they don't know your organization, these experienced professionals know how other companies solve problems. Instead of getting them acculturated to your organization, try switching your orientation and seriously consider how your company could adapt to their ideas.

Meet with these new hires at least biweekly, or better yet, weekly. Let them know how much you are counting on their fresh eyes. Keep telling them how important it is for you to learn their insights about ways things can be improved and mistakes that are being made. When they tell you some, praise them over and over.

Grant them anonymity and license to speak honestly. Encourage them to talk about things they've seen work successfully elsewhere. Listen and explore their views, even when you have doubts about their suggestions. Avoid defending or giving historic justifications for why things are the way they are. Go into these meetings with the goal of reexamining what is and isn't possible in your organization.

Remember, too, that after the first 100 days the newcomers will lose their fresh perspective. By that time they'll have learned the unwritten code of your organization and will become much more guarded in what they say and how they say it. Set a goal of taking advantage of these golden opportunities with each new middle manager you bring in from the outside.

Further, you'll be surprised at how many internal supervisors who are promoted to management can give you an unsullied view of changes that need to be made. Don't neglect them.

Listen to yourself when you begin to defend the status quo or to offer explanations for why certain changes can't be made. These are the very points of weakness that your competitors are hunting for, ones that will give them a competitive advantage. They're working to find ways around the artificial roadblocks and the vested interests that keep you from making innovative changes. You need to search for those same impediments to change and find ways around them.

• *Consultants and other outsiders. Reverence* is a word that's usually linked to people and things that are holy, and that's a good way to think about those who don't "understand" your organization. Outsiders don't know your jargon, acronyms, product lines, or power structure. But they may know a lot about the ways other people have found to solve some of your problems. Revere these outsiders while they go through the process of learning about your organization and its operations.

As a consultant I've often seen people roll their eyes during my first meeting with a new group. When I ask questions they consider dumb and naïve, I almost think I can hear them whispering to one another, "This guy doesn't know anything. This is going to be another waste of time and money." Dealing with that kind of skepticism is part of the cost of being a consultant. But the leader and the whole team should be working to support the outsider as he or she goes through these initial learning phases.

Give outsiders time to work their way through the first three stages of the J Curve in learning about your operation. Once they've mastered the basics, they'll begin to make suggestions and recommendations that can help change your operation and drive efficiency up through Stages 4 and 5.

As a leader, you can help your employees understand the importance of treating outsiders as honored guests. Teach your team members to sympathize with the challenges the outsiders face. Encourage them to do everything possible to make it easy for the nonspecialists to learn about the organization. Use reverence as the standard in judging how well you're treating outsiders. Extending this respect is another way you can create a small world that truly values change and innovation.

EXPERIMENTATION AND EVOLUTION

Once I was invited to the maiden speech by a CEO who had been brought in to turn around a major corporation. Assembled to hear him were 200 important leaders in the organization. Most had high hopes that the company's recent downturn could be reversed, and they were eager to hear the CEO set a new direction. He began by praising past accomplishments but then got down to the basic issue of improving financial operations and raising the share price. As expected, he emphasized cost cutting as a needed but unpopular first step to increasing profitability.

Then he stated that they couldn't grow simply by getting smaller. They would also need to find new ways to add income to the top line. His strategy was not going to be an acquisition binge, he said. Instead, he was counting on these high-powered managers to generate new ideas. "What we need are $200 million ideas," he announced repeatedly. The woman next to me leaned over and whispered, "If I had a $200 million idea, I wouldn't stick around here." She spoke the truth. Most of us if we had an idea that good would be courting venture capital to fund the new enterprise with ourselves as CEO.

Leaders often dream of big ideas that will create a gusher of revenue. But that's rarely how success happens. Instead, most big ideas begin as small ones. Think of Michael Dell starting his business in a dormitory room, Howard Schultz opening one outlet in Seattle, and McDonald's beginning with a single hamburger stand.

Support small experiments. See which ones show promise and redirect resources from the nonperforming ideas into those. Gardening is a good metaphor for this process. You sow many seeds, but then you thin the sprouts and deliver added nutrients and protection to the ones that look as though they'll produce the greatest bounty.

Your main responsibility is to protect these new ideas from the sources of resistance within your own organization. New ideas challenge the status quo. Individuals with strong vested interests will attempt to protect themselves by blocking innovation. You'll probably hear some of this resistance in the initial discussion of a new idea. Those who politely say "*yes...but*" are hunting for problems and for reasons to kill the idea before it gets off the ground. You need to create a small world in which employees focus on what's right about new ideas and then think about how to deal with the challenges.

Many ways can be used to reinforce openness to new ideas. Remind employees that the first form of an idea is never the final form. Everything evolves and changes. "Don't let the ideal destroy the good" is an old adage that captures the wisdom that no idea is perfect. The fact that an idea has a few faults is not necessarily enough of a reason to reject it. The goal of the team is to find what is good and nurture it.

REWARDING INNOVATION

Just as you allocate resources to promising ideas to help them grow, you also need to nurture the growth of the individual or team that's championing the innovation. Public recognition is important for showing your appreciation. These informal rewards can be buttressed with monetary rewards that help signify the importance of each individual's contribution.

The challenge in rewarding such innovators is that it can cause problems with key individuals in the existing management structure. Innovators may be viewed as threats, and the rewards they receive can cause jealousy among those who aren't rewarded.

Resolving these conflicts is your responsibility. You can't avoid the issue and you can't assume the people involved will work it out. If they try to work it out, who do you think will win? Would you bet on someone high up in the existing power structure or a lower-ranking individual with a novel idea? Skilled organizational politicians can claim to endorse a new idea but derail it through benign neglect. The leader must communicate to subordinates that their success depends on fostering the success of innovators.

REMOVING IMPEDIMENTS

Only the leader has the power to block particularly powerful individuals from undermining or sabotaging a new initiative. Offering protection to emerging champions of change is a key attribute of a leader who is creating a culture of change.

You can easily identify the Resisters and can probably name the fault-finders even before the initiative is launched. You can predict who will be passively aggressive by dragging their feet and not fully backing the change. The ones who're living in the past and want to maintain the status quo are easy to spot because that's their "It's a Small World" song, and they sing it over and over.

Meet privately with these key individuals to make certain they know how important it is to you that they support emerging ideas. Help them identify concrete steps they can take to make their support a reality. When they do work to make a new idea a success, be lavish in your praise and rewards. When they don't, try to curtail their influence so they can't undermine the changes. These can be difficult battles. We're often advised to choose our battles carefully. Usually, these conflicts with obstructionists are worth fighting.

PUBLICIZING SUCCESS

Creating a culture of change requires the leader to surround employees with information about all the positive changes that are taking place. At the beginning of this chapter we talked about making workers aware of innovative changes that other companies are making. But it's also important to trumpet internal successes. In addition to using the organization's formal channels of communication, the leader must personally carry the good news from group to group.

The easiest way to do this is by retelling the kinds of success stories described earlier. The leader needs to keep up the drumbeat of change by repeatedly conveying excitement about employees' latest achievements. This is especially important during the early stages of each change initiative. We know from the J Curve that many setbacks will occur at the beginning. The leader has to counteract those failures with news about successes. Remember the upbeat energy of the "It's a Small World" song.

Such communication serves many purposes. It gives workers an overview of success in other departments. It reinforces the more general message that things are changing in the organization. By repeatedly talking about particular change initiatives, the leader reminds employees that he's committed to the change. The implicit message is that the way to win favor with the leader is to support new initiatives.

The leader not only repeats stories of individual accomplishments but he also revels in hearing employees tell him of their successes. Heroes emerge through this process and catchy phrases and slogans too. Listen for words and phrases you can repeat and use as mottoes and hallmarks of the change.

Those singled out for recognition should be the ones who made sacrifices to support the implementation of new ideas, not just those who were the source of the idea. These local heroes can also be recognized during celebrations. Such group events should include the individuals and teams directly responsible for the most recent success as well as groups that need to more actively support the change. Seeing how their coworkers are being honored can be a great incentive to motivate everyone to get behind the change.

It's also important to include the heroes who championed reasonable ideas that didn't yield promised results. These reasonable risks are noble experiments, and those who tried to make them work deserve recognition too. A key part of activation is making it safe for people to make mistakes. These celebrations are ideal for praising those whose efforts to innovate weren't fully successful as well as those whose actions triumphed.

At these celebrations, the leader can use the opportunity to restate the importance of change as a critical value in the organization's culture. At Stages 4 and 5 of the J Curve, employees can appreciate how specific accomplishments reflect the value of change to the organization.

CREATING YOUR SMALL WORLD

It's a long and torturous path to instilling the value of change in the organizational culture. Because the trek is repetitive and barrier-ridden, it requires total commitment. You'll say the same thing over and over again. You'll repeatedly need to reward employees when they do the right thing and correct them when they don't.

If you've raised children, you know the pattern. Teaching values is a continuous and seemingly lifelong process. You have to repeat and repeat, starting when they are toddlers. You do it by rereading books that illustrate the good, extolling their successes when they do the right things, and helping them when they make mistakes. Many days it all seems unending and unachievable. But, like Sisyphus, you must persist.

INDEX

Note: page numbers in **bold** indicate figures

Q

R

About the Author

Jerald M. Jellison, a professor of social psychology at the University of Southern California, created the Business Academy of the Society of Human Resource Management (SHRM) and serves as its dean. He is a sought-after innovator whose insights into organizational change far transcend the classroom. Jellison has been a speaker and consultant to high-profile organizations for more than 25 years; he presents his ideas to thousands each year. He can be reached at:
jellison@usc.edu or **www. jerryjellison.com.**